The School Librarian as
Curriculum Leader

Recent Titles in
Library and Information Science Text Series

Young Adult Literature in Action: A Librarian's Guide, Second Edition
Rosemary Chance

Children's Literature in Action: An Educator's Guide, Second Edition
Sylvia M. Vardell

Internet Technologies and Information Services, Second Edition
Joseph B. Miller

Library Programs and Services: The Fundamentals, Eighth Edition
*G. Edward Evans, Margaret Zarnosky Saponaro, Carol Sinwell,
and Holland Christie*

The Complete Guide to Acquisitions Management, Second Edition
Frances C. Wilkinson, Linda K. Lewis, and Rebecca L. Lubas

Introduction to Cataloging and Classification, Eleventh Edition
Daniel N. Joudrey, Arlene G. Taylor, and David P. Miller

The Collection Program in Schools: Concepts and Practices, Sixth Edition
Marcia A. Mardis

Libraries in the Information Age: An Introduction and Career Exploration,
Third Edition
Denise K. Fourie and Nancy E. Loe

Reference and Information Services: An Introduction, Fifth Edition
Linda C. Smith and Melissa A. Wong, Editors

Guide to the Library of Congress Classification, Sixth Edition
Lois Mai Chan, Sheila S. Intner, and Jean Weihs

Research Methods in Library and Information Science, Sixth Edition
Lynn Silipigni Connaway and Marie L. Radford

Information Services to Diverse Populations: Developing Culturally
Competent Library Professionals
Nicole A. Cooke

THE SCHOOL LIBRARIAN AS CURRICULUM LEADER

Jody K. Howard

Library and Information Science Text Series

LIBRARIES UNLIMITED™

An Imprint of ABC-CLIO, LLC

Santa Barbara, California • Denver, Colorado

Library of Congress Cataloging-in-Publication Data

Names: Howard, Jody K., author.
Title: The school librarian as curriculum leader / Jody K. Howard.
Description: Santa Barbara, California : Libraries Unlimited, an Imprint of
   ABC-CLIO, LLC, 2017. | Series: Library and information science text series |
   Includes bibliographical references and index.
Identifiers: LCCN 2016046003 (print) | LCCN 2017005290 (ebook) | ISBN
   9781598849905 (paperback : acid-free paper) | ISBN 9781440844072 (ebook)
Subjects: LCSH: School libraries—United States. | School librarian participation
   in curriculum planning—United States. | School libraries—Collection
   development—United States. | Libraries and schools—United States. |
   Education—Curricula—United States. | Educational leadership—United
   States. | BISAC: LANGUAGE ARTS & DISCIPLINES / Library & Information
   Science / Collection Development. | LANGUAGE ARTS & DISCIPLINES /
   Library & Information Science / School Media.
Classification: LCC Z675.S3 H6777 2017 (print) | LCC Z675.S3 (ebook) |
   DDC 027.80973—dc23
LC record available at https://lccn.loc.gov/2016046003

ISBN: 978-1-59884-990-5
EISBN: 978-1-4408-4407-2

21 20 19 18 17   1 2 3 4 5

This book is also available as an eBook.

Libraries Unlimited
An Imprint of ABC-CLIO, LLC

ABC-CLIO, LLC
130 Cremona Drive, P.O. Box 1911
Santa Barbara, California 93116-1911
www.abc-clio.com

This book is printed on acid-free paper ∞

Manufactured in the United States of America

This book is dedicated to my father, Richard F. Howard, who instilled in me the love of research and writing; to my two sons, Joseph B. Hanson and William H. Hanson, who listened to my incessant conversations about school librarians; my sisters, Vicki Leyba, Debbie Vanderlinde, and Teri Parsons who have also supported me in this venture. A special thanks goes to Teri for providing me with a teacher's viewpoint on the role of the school librarian and assisted in editing this manuscript.

This text is also dedicated to the school library students and practitioners who have shared with me their experiences, successes, and challenges in working as school librarians in our current education environment. Their leadership abilities, commitment, and dedication to the school library profession stimulates the growth and creation of knowledge for the members of their learning communities. Thank you!

Contents

Introduction

Today the American Association of School Librarians (AASL) (2009) identifies five roles for the school librarian: Instructional Partner, Information Specialist, Teacher, Program Administrator, and Leader. The focus of most of these roles is working with the students, faculty members, staff, administrators, and other members of the learning community. One common denominator of each of the five roles is curriculum which is the basis of any school program, and school librarians must be knowledgeable of this concept and understand how to be leaders in this area. Each of the five roles addresses some aspect of the curriculum of the school.

A school librarian's days are filled with collaborating, planning, instructing, working on the leadership team, and providing each student access to the information they need. Little time is left to really administer the program or build the foundation upon which an exciting school library program should be built. Part of this foundation includes developing access to resources for students enhancing their abilities to continue with their learning. This foundation includes knowing and organizing those resources to provide a seamless path from question to answer for each student. It also includes assisting students in creating knowledge based on the answers to their questions. The school librarian so often in the forefront of working with the members of the learning community, must allot time working behind the scenes to learn about the curriculum, develop collections based on this knowledge, and to provide access to these collections.

This purpose of this book is to present information to instructors working with pre-service school library students to become effective leaders in the area of curriculum. The book can also be used by practicing librarians wishing to hone their skills in the curriculum area.

The text provides a journey into all aspects of the world of curriculum with an overview of the processes of developing a vibrant collection and meshing these processes with the roles of information Specialist and Instructional Partner. The chapters address basic concepts needed to work with faculty and students providing access to just the right resources among the thousands that are available in the collection. The text also provides tips on how to work with faculty to determine what resources are needed to address the national, state, and local standards facing educational institutions. In addition, each chapter identifies reflective questions that will provoke discussion and assist in developing one's own personal philosophy of how to develop a vibrant school library program. Each chapter addresses a different aspect of how to use curriculum to become a dynamic school librarian.

CHAPTER 1: WHAT IS CURRICULUM?

Chapter 1 provides a definition of curriculum and identifies how the definition is used in different educational settings. The national and state standards are identified and discussed.

CHAPTER 2: WHAT IS CURRICULUM LEADERSHIP?

This chapter discusses the concept of leadership and aligns the leadership concept with the roles of the school librarian. Various models of leadership are explained.

CHAPTER 3: SCHOOL CULTURE AND SCHOOL RELATIONSHIPS

To be successful in a school, one needs to understand the different forces present in the school. These forces make up the culture of an organization and this culture impacts the workings of that organization. School librarians must understand this culture in order to develop relationships with other members of the faculty.

CHAPTER 4: CURRICULUM MAPPING

Curriculum mapping is one of the skills school librarians need to develop to determine what curriculum is being presented in the classrooms. This chapter provides specific guidelines for developing a curriculum map.

CHAPTER 5: COLLECTION MAPPING

Collection mapping provides the school librarians with knowledge of the collection in the library so that these resources may be aligned with the curriculum maps. The chapter presents specific guidelines for developing a collection map.

CHAPTER 6: COLLECTION DEVELOPMENT

Collection development should be based on the curriculum maps and the collection maps that the school librarian developed. This chapter illustrates how a collection development plan is constructed to be used to create an all-inclusive school library collection.

CHAPTER 7: INSTRUCTIONAL PARTNER AND CHANGE

This chapter identifies the challenges school librarians face in implementing their role as an instructional partner. This chapter presents various models of the change process with tips on how school librarians can implement change.

CHAPTER 8: THE LEARNING COMMUNITY

Chapter 8 explains the concept of a learning community along with various configurations of learning communities. Educational institutions function with different types of learning communities and school librarians should have the background and knowledge of each of these types.

CHAPTER 9: TEACHER AND SCHOOL LIBRARIAN PARTNERSHIP

Teachers and school librarians must work together as partners and Chapter 9 provides information on how this can be accomplished. Guided inquiry, essential questions, and implementation of state and national standards are explored.

CHAPTER 10: BEYOND THE SCHOOL

School librarians should be a force of nature and their influence needs to extend beyond their own schools. This chapter identifies ways they can make an impact at the local, state, and national levels.

The school librarian's role in all aspects of curriculum is essential to create an environment where students can flourish. Using the concepts and guidelines presented in this text, school librarians will be able to navigate the journey becoming a powerful and influential leader and establishing an effective school library program.

Chapter 1

What Is Curriculum?

At the conclusion of this chapter, the reader will be able to define curriculum and discuss the concept of a curriculum philosophy, identify curriculum standards, including the national and state standards, the American Association of School Librarian Standards (AASL), the International Society for Technology in Education (ISTE) Standards, and the Standards for the 21st-Century Learner. The goal is for the reader to grasp the relationship of the standards to the curriculum of the school and the school library program.

Curriculum is a word that anyone—student, instructor, parent, administrator, or taxpayer—has used many times and in many different contexts. Each of these contexts provides a different slant to the meaning of the word. Curriculum theory, curriculum development, curriculum framework, curriculum mapping, curriculum standards, and curriculum program are a few of the common phrases. Curriculum in early Latin comes from a race course or to run a race (Hamilton, Gibbons, & Brill, 1980; Wilson, 2016). This metaphor helps visualize the breadth of curriculum as the runners must be aware of the distance, the time, the layout of the course, the turns, the directional signs, and the water stations. A race has many different parts all working together for one goal and so does the concept and implementation of curriculum.

In a K-12 setting, curriculum is used to describe a syllabus for a course, teacher-prepared lessons, the scope of the subject matter, or the sequence of the materials taught. Curriculum includes the pedagogical methods used to present the course, the duration of the course, the resources needed, and can describe commercially produced programs addressing a specific subject area. Curriculum is an all-encompassing term that describes different aspects of the educational process (Eisenberg & Berkowitz, 1988).

To be curriculum leaders, school librarians must have a complete understanding of the concept of curriculum and its relationship to the school. This chapter will provide an overview of this concept and its relationship to the K-12 arena. This overview will examine the basic tenets of curriculum philosophy and the practical nature of the relationship of curriculum to the standards movement.

OVERVIEW OF CURRICULUM

Defining curriculum is a difficult task as the concept is broad, has changed, and been revised throughout the last century (Wiles & Bondi, 2010). Wilson (2016) summarizes 11 overall types of curricula used in schools today. Glatthorn, Boschee, and Whitehead (2009) identify 15 scholars since the 1900s who define curriculum from different points of view. These definitions range from curriculum as a prescribed set of materials that each student learns during their K-12 education to statements that include all events occurring during the school day, either while students are in class or simply on the school grounds. The definitions of curriculum create a continuum between the prescriptive concepts on one end to the all-inclusive experiences that students encounter as learners. Lunenburg (2011) examines curriculum as content, learning experiences, objectives, specific plans, and through a broader philosophical approach that he identifies as nontechnical. These different educational beliefs run the gamut on the curriculum continuum. It is important for school librarians to reflect on what they believe curriculum includes based on their experiences and study, the culture of their school districts, and the direction of their individual schools.

CURRICULUM PHILOSOPHY

Everyone involved in education has a philosophy whether this is reflected in a written statement or is simply a deep-seated idea that clarifies the roles of schools and education in a student's life. Professionals are often asked what their philosophy of education is, and they usually have a formal written statement. Those people not involved in education may not have a formal written statement, but each taxpayer can offer an opinion of what is important for students in today's schools. As school library professionals and curriculum leaders, it is necessary that we understand our own beliefs about education and those of the school district in which we work. The curriculum philosophy creates a path to the end product of helping students learn. Practitioners often do not see the relevance of studying curriculum philosophy; however, understanding different beliefs assists educators in determining which curriculum proposals to implement, helps identify best practices, and guides school reform (Glatthorn, Boschee, & Whitehead, 2009).

Scholars have organized the philosophies and theories of curriculum in a variety of ways (Beauchamp, 1975; Bradley, 2004; Lunenburg, 2011; Oliva, 2009; Schiro, 2008; Tanner and Tanner, 2007). Schiro (2008) presents an all-inclusive, but manageable, delineation of the different types of curriculum philosophies or ideologies. He aligns current educational thought in four different categories based on the purpose of education. The first category is the *Scholar Academic* ideology. This ideology steeps the curriculum in a content area providing the students with sufficient skills and knowledge to master the desired content. The *Social Efficiency* ideology bases the school curriculum on the learning skills necessary to prepare students to be good citizens. This philosophy aims to help students become well-adapted citizens able to live worthwhile lives and, in the process, influence the social norms and practices of society. The *Learner Centered* philosophy concentrates on the individual needs of the student, focusing on the skills and knowledge necessary for these students to grow and develop into independent, well-adjusted individuals. The *Social Reconstruction* ideology focuses on students developing as many problem-solving skills as possible to eliminate some of the basic challenges of our society and, in the process, to create a better society for all individuals. Schiro's four categories synthesize and organize the plethora of individual curriculum explanations from different scholars in the field. Each of these philosophies has a different history and is focused on different ways of looking at curriculum. The goals differ in providing content, increasing skills, developing the individual learner, and creating a better society. All four ideologies have the learner as the focus. Having knowledge of Schiro's ideologies is important for the current school librarian as his framework organizes the vast area of curriculum into sizable sections with each section having the learner as the focus.

Lunenburg (2011) categorizes curriculum as content, learning experiences, objectives, instructional plans, and nontechnical approaches. His framework is a progressive one that has each category interdependent on the next category. The content category includes the subject matter to be presented to the student. The learning experiences connect with the student's backgrounds and relate how these experiences have shaped their lives echoing John Dewey's concept of learning (1938). In Lunenburg's (2011) framework behavioral objectives are important and he aligns them with Bloom's taxonomy (Bloom, 1956). All three of these categories are reflected in a curriculum plan. Lunenburg (2011) expands the common instructional plan to include additional ideas that are nontechnical, which could include a hidden curriculum or the null curriculum explained later.

In examining the brief description of Schiro's (2008) and Lunenburg's (2011) philosophies, the challenge of understanding the world of curriculum becomes evident. The different theories and philosophies of education are vast in number and reflect different viewpoints surrounding the issues. The common themes of both viewpoints are content, experiences, and the learner. These themes hold true with other philosophies and theories.

CURRICULUM COMPONENTS

Curriculum is an all-encompassing word that has many different parts. Some of the most common ideas of curriculum are its overall definition, focus, and implementation. At the national, state, and district levels, the words associated with curriculum are content knowledge, accreditation, assessment, standards, and student growth. At the school level, the focus words include these same words but also take into account the classroom processes. These words should be added to the vocabulary: lesson plans, groupings, and collaboration. Classroom teachers must look at the scope of their curriculum to understand what the students learned before arriving in their classrooms and what they need to know before continuing on the academic ladder. Students need to understand the process and concept of addition before they tackle long division. Studying World War II before studying World War I will not present a logical sequence of events on the historical timeline. All of these parts of curriculum are tangible, and state and national educators, district administrators, and classroom teachers are inundated with information they need to function successfully in their positions.

Two types of curriculum that are at times overlooked are hidden curriculum and null curriculum (Oliva, 2009; Tanner & Tanner, 2007; and Wilson, 2016). Hidden curriculum refers to what the students learn that is not part of the established curriculum. Null curriculum is the content missing from the prescribed course of study.

Hidden Curriculum

Hidden curriculum looks at the organizational structure and culture of the school. This curriculum embodies all of the processes and cultural rituals that students experience in their schools outside of the required content. Longstreet and Shane (1993) address a hidden curriculum students learn from the messages they receive outside of planned activities. This hidden curriculum includes the classroom management techniques of each instructor: raising one's hand before speaking; desks in a straight row; desks clustered in different configurations; and other rules and regulations in specific classrooms. Do students need a pass to leave the classroom or do they have free or unfettered reign of the building? Is the high school campus a closed campus where students must remain at school for the entire day or are students allowed to go to the local fast-food restaurant for lunch? Are there consequences if a student is late for class? While answering these questions, consider what message the school is sending to students; what hidden curriculum is present? Tanner and Tanner (2007), believing that historically the term "hidden" elicits a negative connotation, describe this curriculum as collateral as it is the by-product of what students learn outside of the overt, or planned, content curriculum.

Null Curriculum

Null curriculum refers to the content that is not taught or that is left out of the written curriculum. What is missing from the curriculum content that is presented? In a history class are only certain events in history presented? Is the slant or focus from one point of view with other points of view eliminated? Students learn from the subjects that are presented in a structured manner, and they also learn from what is missing from the curriculum. This null curriculum is often discussed in the area of multiculturalism or diversity (Oliva, 2009). A concrete example of the presence of null curriculum may be found in the school library. What books are displayed? Are there books with diverse people on the cover? Is one race or group of people notably missing from the items displayed? What is this teaching students and adults in the school? Is the absence of certain books in the library collection speaking to students in a negative way?

The concept of curriculum has expanded from its use in the early days of the United States. In her seminal work, Taba (1962) defines curriculum as a structured plan related to the materials developed by the teachers melded with the learning experiences presented to the students. Today, this definition has evolved to include not just the planned activities, but the abovementioned hidden curriculum, the null curriculum, the concepts the students learn, and the accountability process that is in place through the standards movement (Wiles & Bondi, 2010).

EDUCATIONAL REFORM—OVERVIEW

With the publication of *A Nation at Risk* report in 1983, the need for educational reform was catapulted into public view (Barton, 2009). In 1994, the Clinton administration reauthorized the Elementary and Secondary Education Act (ESEA) and through this a standards-based mandate was enacted into federal law (Shepard, Hannaway, & Baker, 2009). The 2001 No Child Left Behind Act (NCLB) evolved from ESEA and required states to develop and implement standards that would raise student achievement in the schools (Barton, 2009). NCLB, although a federal mandate, placed the requirements for developing these content standards on the states. The face of education has changed since the enactment of NCLB. In December 2015, President Obama signed the Every Student Succeeds Act (ESSA) with the intent of providing every child regardless of their backgrounds the means to succeed and fulfill their destinies (U.S. Department of Education, 2015). These legislative actions have impacted the districts, schools, classroom teachers, school librarians, and students.

STANDARDS

A by-product of these legislative actions is the development of standards and outcomes that will illustrate a student's growth from year to year. These standards provide a pathway to measure the increase in student achievement. Since 1994 standards have been developed in all 50 states (Orlich, 2011), but these documents and the means to implement and assess these standards have evolved in different directions and with different outcomes. Shepherd, Hannaway, and Baker (2009) discuss the challenge of looking at both content and the assessment of that content. State level products have been created as well as products on the national level. One movement that has gained traction is the development of the Common Core Standards that has been supported by the Common Core Standards Initiative developed in 2011 (LaVenia, Cohen-Vogel & Lang, 2015). Although initially supported by many states, some states have reconsidered their support of this initiative. An important point is that both at the national and state level, movements occur with the goal of increasing the academic prowess of each student. The common components are: Standards and Assessments.

As the content standards have evolved, so have the standards affecting the school library. In 1998 the American Association of School Librarians (AASL) developed the Information Literacy Standards for Student Learning that guided the school librarian as an instructional partner and as an information specialist (American Association of School Librarians [AASL] & Association of Educational and Communications Technology [AECT], 1998). These standards provided a pathway to collaborating with classroom teachers to assist students in becoming information literate. In 2007 AASL revised these standards into the *Standards for the 21st-Century Learner*. These standards not only addressed the skills necessary for the twenty-first century learner but also identified the dispositions in action, the responsibilities of the students, and provided self-assessment strategies. In 2015 AASL began the revision of these standards. As with the national organizations developing the content standards for their discipline, AASL has developed the standards for working with students to develop their inquiry and research skills.

One notable difference between the 1998 information literacy standards and the 2007 standards for the twenty-first-century learner is in the area of literacy. *Empowering Learners: Guidelines for School Library Programs* (AASL, 2009) expanded the definition of literacy to include a variety of literacies: media, visual, technology, and information literacy. To prepare students for the twenty-first century, school librarians have the responsibility to assist them in developing all of these literacies.

One aspect of working with students in the area of research is using any available tool that will assist them in finding needed information. Therefore, the school librarian should be aware of the information technology standards developed by the International Society of Technology in Education (ISTE). This nonprofit organization has taken the lead in developing these standards for students, teachers, administrators, coaches, and computer science educators (ISTE, 2016). In some schools, a technology person is a member of the staff and works with the school librarian. In other schools, this responsibility rests with the school librarian. In each case, the school librarian needs to be aware of these standards and well versed in their implementation.

Another organization that addresses standards and has developed a framework is the Partnership for 21st Century Learning (P21 Partnership for 21st Century Learning, n.d.). This organization was developed in 2002 as a coalition to bring together members of the business community and education, as well as policy makers. Its purpose was to develop a set of standards that described the skills students will need to succeed and achieve in the world of the twenty-first century. The goal was membership of all 50 states so the coalition would gain traction in this movement. The framework for 21st Century Learning provided content knowledge, learning and innovation skills, information, media and technology skills, and life and career skills. Many states still remain as part of this coalition and provide input into the framework and the means of implementing it.

WHAT DOES ALL OF THIS MEAN?

The purpose of this chapter is to provide an overview of the parameters of the curriculum in K-12 schools. The definition of curriculum is different for every person. School librarians by virtue of their positions are involved in the entire curriculum of the school and must work with all students and teachers to implement the content standards and the standards for the twenty-first century learner. School librarians must articulate their definition of curriculum and determine how this definition aligns with the culture and curriculum of the school. By doing this, the school librarian and the staff will watch the students succeed in their quest for knowledge.

Reflective Questions

This chapter discussed two different philosophical views on curriculum, those of Schiro and of Lunenburg. Which philosophy resonates with your beliefs?

What is your philosophy of education?

What is your definition of curriculum?

What is the null curriculum in your school?

What is the hidden curriculum in your school?

How do you plan to align the Standards for the 21st Century Learner with the content standards being implemented in your school?

Chapter 2

What Is Curriculum Leadership?

At the conclusion of this chapter, the reader will have been exposed to the concept of leadership and the existence of leadership theories. The reader will understand the relationship of leadership to the area of curriculum and will be knowledgeable about the leadership role of the school librarian as an information specialist and instructional partner.

Recently when discussing the concept of leadership, a colleague told of an event that happened many years ago when she was in high school. One of the teachers became aware that she was transferring to a new school for her senior year and the teacher indicated this was a shame. The teacher had identified my friend as a leader whom she was hoping would run for class president during her senior year. When asked why this was a memory that remained fresh in her mind, my colleague replied that prior to this time she had not considered herself a leader and was not really sure what the teacher saw that identified her as having leadership qualities. This event caused my colleague to reflect on how she is a leader and how that has impacted her professional career and her personal life. Just what did that teacher know about my colleague that made her think she was a leader?

The concept of leadership is intangible and elusive. If a room full of people were asked to identify a person they consider a leader, each person could describe someone, be it a well-recognized historical figure such as Franklin Delano Roosevelt, a current politician or screen star, or one's own mother, father, teacher, or friend. When asked why they consider this person to be a leader, again the responses would be varied. Just as my colleague's teacher recognized her leadership qualities, each of us could describe a leader and identify the qualities that establish that person as a leader. It is much more difficult to define the concept and to evaluate ourselves as leaders. In this chapter we will examine the concept of leadership and how it impacts our roles as school librarians.

WHY LEADERSHIP?

Standards for school library programs have been in existence since the early 1900s (AASL, 2009). These standards have influenced the creation of school libraries and have guided the school librarian on the path to implementing an effective school library program. The concept of leadership has been implied in the standards since the 1970s (Haycock, 1991) and leadership responsibilities are found in both *Information Power: Guidelines for School Library Media Programs* (American Association of School Librarians [AASL] & [AECT], 1988) and *Information Power: Building Partnerships for Learning* (AASL & AECT, 1998). In both *Information Powers*, leadership was not listed as a primary role of the school librarian. In 2009 with the publication of *Empowering Learners, Guidelines for the School Library Program* (AASL, 2009), leadership has been established as one of the specific roles of the school librarian. Leadership is an essential component in establishing an effective school library program. It is fitting as we begin to look at our role as curriculum leaders that we reflect on what leadership is and how we can develop our leadership skills. School librarians should understand leadership as a global concept and understand and identify how they are leaders, what skills they possess, and how they can strengthen their personal leadership skills.

WHAT IS LEADERSHIP?

The concept of leadership has been evident since the early days of history. Bass and Bass (2008) use the structure of the family unit as an example. Children see the leadership of their parents and begin to understand how a unit works together and moves forward as a unit. Bennis and Nanus (2003) indicate that there are more than 850 definitions of the term leadership. Many of these definitions have not withstood the test of time. Many of them describe the qualities that make a leader. Many of them ignore the definition altogether and focus on how to train employees to be leaders. Woolls (1990) uses a simple but very clear definition of leadership that refers to the verb form of the word, lead. Leadership is the ability to guide and move people in a certain direction. Leaders are able to influence others to follow them in the direction they are going. One question that has been often debated is: Are leaders born or made? Some leaders have natural talents and abilities, and others have developed the necessary traits to influence those who are following them. Reflecting on this question will generate good information for the school librarian and may possibly be answered in the affirmative for both. Yes, some leaders are born; yes, some leaders are made.

Various schools of thought have evolved around the concept of leadership. Bolden, Gosling, Marturano, and Dennison (2003) present a clear delineation of how to categorize these different schools of thought. They look at leadership through the eyes of the great man theories, trait theories, behavioral theories, situational leadership, contingency theory, transactional theory, and transformational theory. Covey (2004) presents a similar list of leadership theories complete with the researchers associated with this concept. Similar to

Bolden et al. (2003), Kilburg and Donohue (2011) have identified major approaches to leadership theory including such theories as the charismatic theory, the effectiveness/outcome theory, and the ethical/moral theory.

None of these lists is all inclusive in identifying the existing leadership theories. At the present time, this would be impossible to do as leadership can be analyzed in a variety of ways. If leadership is scrutinized from the potential leader's point of view, one theory can be developed. Analyzing this theory would not take into account the effect of the followers' actions on the leader's performance (Kilburg & Donohue, 2011). Nor would it take into consideration the culture of the organization and its impact on the leader's performance (Howard, 2010a). As school librarians reflect on their leadership qualities and behaviors, their knowledge that there are so many different theories, concepts, and models of looking at leadership will assist them in understanding how difficult of a task this may be. Looking at a few of the most common theories will provide school librarians with a place to start this journey. The following list of leadership theories provides a foundational overview of leadership concepts: McGregor (1985), Bass (1985), Kouzes and Posner (2002), Bennis (2009, 2003), Bennis & Nanus (2003), and Sheldon (1991).

McGregor

Douglas McGregor developed a concept of leadership and management that exemplifies the behavioral school of thinking (Bolden, Gosling, Marturano, Dennison, 2003). He did not isolate the traits that leaders possessed; instead, he assessed these skills through the interactions with individuals. He identified Theory X and Theory Y (McGregor, 1985). These concepts described the leader's assumptions concerning human behavior. Theory X managers assume that the average human being has an inherent dislike for work and will avoid it at all costs. Because of this, the employees will need to be coerced into working, controlled, directed, and will face the consequences of their actions if they do not fulfill the responsibilities of their jobs. Theory Y managers assume that workers were self-directed and committed to the goals of the organization. Workers are eager to exercise their creativity, imagination, and ingenuity to perform their job-related tasks. McGregor identified Theory X managers as ones who needed to control their workers to accomplish the necessary goals. Theory Y managers worked with their employees in a collaborative manner and, through integrating the talents of the workers, were able to affect innovation in their organizations. McGregor described two types of leaders through the Theory X and the Theory Y concepts. Leaders believing that workers are in the Theory X category will be hierarchical types of leaders; leaders believing that the employees represent Theory Y, will lead with a collaborative integrative style.

Bass: Transactional and Transformational Theory

James McGregor Burns (1978) is credited with creating the terms transactional and transformational leadership, and Bass (1985) has further clarified them. Transactional leadership is often explained as the traditional type of leadership that has the structure of the leader rewarding followers (Howell & Avolio, 1993). In this model, the leader and the followers agree upon tasks that the followers should complete. When the followers complete the tasks, they receive an extrinsic reward because they have fulfilled the requirements of the assigned task. This contingent reward leadership (Brymer & Gray, 2006) involves both active and positive exchanges between the leader and the followers, but the leader may interact with the follower at any time during the follower's work, or the leader may choose to wait until the follower has completed the task and then discuss the process and progress of the follower. In this type of leadership, the follower completes the assigned task but only the assigned task. The follower's creativity and initiative are stifled when using the transactional model. As long as the leader and the follower are happy with this relationship, then work will progress and the tasks will be completed. Transformational leadership, however, extends beyond setting goals for specific rewards. It has been labeled charismatic leadership (Chemers, 1997; Howell & Avolio, 1993) and allows the follower to break the bonds of performance for a specific reward. In the transformational model, the leader encourages the followers to develop their creativity, problem solve the task at hand, and succeed in their work through their desire to help improve the organization. Followers catch the spirit of the leader's vision; because the followers believe in this vision, they do all they can to promote it. The problems that the leader presents to the followers encourage the followers to create solutions that will move the organization forward through implementing the vision of the leader. The vision of the leader and the followers are one and the same. Leaders stimulate, support, encourage, and assist the followers in developing their own self-interests, which support the mission of the organization. Followers receive their own intrinsic rewards for the work they accomplish.

Bass (1985) conducted research in this leadership area and developed a tool to measure the presence of leadership. Bass's research consisted of open-ended information discussions with 70 executives attending a training workshop. Bass wanted to know what qualities and characteristics the leaders possessed when they were able to convince followers to abandon their own desires to support the leader's vision. Working with this and further data collection, Bass and Avolio (1990) developed a multifactor leadership questionnaire (MLQ) (Chemers, 1997). This MLQ can be used to determine if a leader is a transactional leader, a transformational leader, or a leader who is actually a non-leader or one who exhibits a laissez-faire behavior where leadership is absent. Through factor analysis, Bass and Avolio (1990) developed their leadership model to identify transactional leadership (rewards and management by exception), and transformational leadership (charisma, inspirational motivation, intellectual stimulation, and individualized consideration).

Two additional leadership theories by Kouzes and Posner (2002) and Warren Bennis (2003) were developed for use in the business field that reflected some of the tenets of transactional leadership. Although these leadership models were developed for the business field, they are applicable to the information science field. In fact, Kouzes and Posner have revised their leadership practices inventory to include appropriate questions for a variety of fields outside of business. They have done extensive work in the field of education and also with students.

Kouzes and Posner: The Leadership Challenge

One widely publicized and useful area of research about leadership is the work of James Kouzes and Barry Posner (2002), who conducted their original research in the 1980s. As instructors in the School of Business at Santa Clara University, they began collecting qualitative and quantitative data determining common characteristics that leaders possess. Their data collection consisted of in-depth interviews, some lasting from one hour to four or five hours, initial surveys, and extensive follow-up surveys of 12 pages in length and consisting of 38 open-ended questions. These surveys were given to over 350,000 people during the 1980s. Their website, www.lpionline.com, presents the statistical data showing the reliability and validity of the data that were collected. Kouzes and Posner assumed that if they asked ordinary people how they had accomplished extraordinary events, the resulting data would provide a model that could prepare people to assume leadership roles. From these data, Kouzes and Posner identified the following patterns that illustrated effective leadership: Model the Way; Inspire a Shared Vision; Challenge the Process; Enable Others to Act; and Encourage the Heart. In addition to these five best practices, the authors developed Ten Commitments to Leadership that are embedded in the five practices. The Ten Commitments clarified the five practices:

- Model the Way explains the process leaders use who to manifest examples of leadership by how they live and work. The commitment to Model the Way encourages leaders to understand their personal values and to explain and implement them as shared values.

- Inspire a Shared Vision, is just that. Leaders explain their vision of leadership as clearly as possible and then encourage others to accept this vision.

- Challenge the Process addresses the needs of leaders to take risks, challenge the status quo, and, by doing so, improve the organization.

- Enable Others to Act is the process leaders use that encourages others to follow them and support others as they start on the leadership journey.

- Encourage the Heart is the process leaders use to recognize the contributions made by members of the organization. This leadership practice supports the celebration of individual and team success within the organization.

Kouzes and Posner's research supports leaders acting as role models, creating and sharing a vision, pushing the envelope when necessary, assisting others in becoming leaders, and celebrating other's successes. In addition to these five best practices, the authors developed Ten Commitments to Leadership that are embedded in the five practices. The Ten Commitments further clarified the five practices.

Kouzes and Posner (2009) subsequently developed a Leadership Practices Inventory (LPI) that determines the leadership qualities one possesses and assists respondents in determining what they need to improve or develop to become an effective leader. Their 30 years of research, available on their website (http://www.leadershipchallenge.com/About-section-Our-Approach.aspx), supports the idea that using the data from the LPI to increase one's leadership skills will give better results in a person's work and personal relationships. The LPI is readily accessible and a tool that novice and veteran leaders can use to determine what they should accomplish to increase their leadership influence.

Bennis

A fourth influential leadership guru is Warren G. Bennis. Bennis, a prolific writer in the field of leadership and management, founded the Leadership Institute at the University of Southern California (USC) and was a distinguished professor of Business Administration at USC until his death in 2014 (Rifkin, 2014). Although Bennis has written extensively, his two seminal works are: *Leaders: Strategies for Taking Charge* published in 1985 with Burt Nanus and *On Becoming a Leader* first published in 1989. Bennis and Nanus believed leadership is a necessary ingredient for successful organizations. Leaders must help organizations develop new visions and then mobilize their members to implement these visions. To prove their assumption, they conducted 90 interviews and a series of observations with 60 CEOs of corporations and 30 with leaders in the public sector. Because their subjects in this research were established leaders, the focus of the research was on how the leaders had constructed their positions of leadership and developed their roles to lead their organizations. From this qualitative data, four themes emerged that comprised Bennis and Nanus's leadership model. Bennis and Nanus identified these themes as strategies and they addressed having a vision, communication, trust, and positive self-regard.

Bennis continued building on these four strategies with additional qualitative research in *On Becoming a Leader* (2003). In this work, Bennis illustrated how the leaders actually become leaders and how they lead. Bennis compared it to how a person recognizes beauty. Beauty is hard to define, but one knows beauty when one sees it (xxvi). With this thought in mind, Bennis believed that additional research should be conducted by analyzing specific leaders. He believed that a paradigm of leadership is based on leaders and how they act in their work, not on specific leadership theories. In *On Becoming a Leader*, Bennis describes 30 people who are leaders in many different positions. He interviewed individuals such as Gloria Steinem, female activist; Norman Lear, television writer-producer; Herb Alpert, musician; and Gloria Anderson, newspaper editor. All of these people are leaders in specifically different areas, and they all exhibit four leadership competencies: create a shared vision; have self-confidence and the ability to reflect that self-confidence to others; have integrity; and have adaptive capacity that allows them to handle change in an intelligent manner. The research in *Leaders* (1989) analyzed the identified leaders and described how they exhibited their leadership competencies. In the research for *On Becoming a Leader*, Bennis increased his data collection of how people become leaders and how they lead their corporations. Bennis allows readers of his works to draw their own conclusions as to how they should become leaders in their own areas of expertise.

Brooke Sheldon

Much of Bennis's influence was in the business world but his books and works can be applied to every aspect of leadership, regardless of the organization. One direct connection to the information professional is through the work of Brooke Sheldon (1991). Sheldon replicated Bennis's research in the library field by interviewing 60 library professionals. Because Bennis had conducted his studies with an emphasis on corporate leaders, Sheldon wanted to see if library leaders had the same leadership qualities. Sheldon wanted to determine if leaders in the library and information science field possessed the same qualities (p. 2). Do leaders in different disciplines possess the same leadership qualities?

Sheldon (1991) used some of the same questions Bennis used regarding strengths and weaknesses, significant decision points in a person's life and influential life events. She also added a question concerning mentors and asked the participants what their view of the future was. Her criteria for her interviewees limited the participants to a director of a major public or academic library, a nationally recognized school librarian, executive director of one of the major library organizations (SLA, ALA, ARL, etc.), dean of a library school (selected by peers), or a state librarian (pp. 3–4). Sheldon concluded that the library leaders mirrored the four strategies identified by Bennis and Nanus (1985). In regards to the two additional questions Sheldon asked, she found that all but two of the participants had mentors who had been instrumental in helping them in their professional lives. In addition, the participants in Sheldon's study supported emphasizing the qualities of creativity, risk taking, innovation, and intuition as leadership criteria. Sheldon's research provides a direct link from Bennis's leadership theory to the information professional.

All of these frameworks examine ways to think about leadership and provide elements to consider as one reflects on one's own leadership characteristics and style. Each of them provides information to reflect on as one is traveling on the leadership journey. (See Table 2.1.)

PERSONAL LEADERSHIP SKILLS

Analyzing leadership as a global concept is important, but it is equally important for school librarians to understand the leadership skills they already possess and to determine how they can develop and expand these skills. It is imperative that school librarians understand their personality types as this will provide the self-awareness necessary for any leader. Understanding themselves will assist school librarians in determining what needs to be accomplished to continue developing as a leader. Three of the common methods to assess one's personality type and to determine one's personal leadership traits or skills are: The Myers Briggs Trait Inventory, Enneagrams, and Kouzes and Posner's LPI survey.

Myers-Briggs Type Indicator (MBTI)

In the early 1900s, Carl G. Jung confirmed that individuals have specific personality types and mental preferences for how they act, just as individuals have

Table 2.1 Selective Leadership Frameworks

McGregor (1985) Theory X and Theory Y

Theory X—Leaders assume followers dislike work and will do anything to avoid it.

Theory Y—Leaders assume that followers are self-directed and committed to the organization.

Bass (1985) Transactional and Transformational Theory

Transactional—Leader directs followers and rewards their efforts.

Transformational—Leader directs followers but encourages them to use their own creativity to reach the stated goal.

Kouzes and Posner (2002) The Leadership Challenge

Organized around Five Practices and Ten Commitments

Model the Way

Inspire a Shared Vision

Challenge the Process

Enable Others to Act

Encourage the Heart

Bennis and Nanus (1985, 1997, 2003)

Organized through four strategies: Having a vision; being able to communicate; inspiring trust; and having positive self-regard.

Bennis (1989, 2009)

Identified four leadership competencies: Creating a shared vision; having self-confidence; integrity; and adaptive capacity to handle change.

Sheldon (1991)

Replicated Bennis's research with information professionals.

Added additional questions about mentoring and the vision of the future.

---

physical preferences such as using the right or left hands and the dominance of one eye. In the 1940s two of his students, Isabel Briggs Myers and her mother, Katharine C. Briggs, elaborated on his theory of personality and developed a psychometric questionnaire called the Myers-Briggs Type Indicator (Kennedy & Kennedy, 2004). Myers and Briggs believed that the purpose of this questionnaire was to identify and measure personality preferences. After completing this test, the participants better understand themselves and the type of personalities that make them who they are (Myers, 1998).

Myers believed that a person's mental activity relied on perception and judgment and these qualities influenced how a person acts. Perception influences how a person views a situation and judgment reflects how they then act (Myers, 1980, p. 1). Leaders will be more effective if they understand themselves and their personality preferences better. Sometimes while working with others, someone will say, "Draw me a picture as I am really a visual learner." This self-knowledge helps each of us understand the most effective way that we learn. The MBTI will help a person gain this knowledge.

The MBTI now consists of a series of multiple-choice questions that require the participant to decide on one of the choices listed. The MBTI measures three personality types suggested by Jung: extraversion-introversion, sensing-intuition, thinking and feeling. Briggs and Myers added a fourth element that measures judgment-perception (Myers & Myers, 1995). Extraversion-introversion identifies where a person focuses their attention. People who prefer extroversion focus their attention on other people and things outside of themselves. Introverts focus on the world of ideas and impressions. Sensing and intuition describe how a person assimilates information. Sensing individuals use their five senses to acquire information. People who prefer using intuition look at the big picture and acquire information through patterns. Thinking and feeling address how people make decisions. Thinking people rely on logic and objective analysis; feeling people rely on values and subjective ideas that are part of their nature. Judging and perceiving addresses how people interact with the world outside of themselves. Judging people like a structured, planned, and organized approach to life and how they address problems. Perceiving individuals are flexible and spontaneous, approaching life in an unstructured manner. Upon completing the inventory, the participants receive a report that lists their preferences in each of the dimensions mentioned above as a combination of letters (Myers & Briggs Foundation, 2016).

Enneagram Framework

The Enneagram psychological typology is an old philosophical framework that has been used successfully as a self-assessment tool (Schreiber & Shannon, 1998). The Enneagram is based on an age-old theory having its beginnings in Afghanistan (Matise, 2007). This self-assessment is a personality model divided into nine different personality types. The Enneagram presents a series of paired statements, and the respondents are forced to choose the statement in each pair that best describes themselves, even though in some cases it will be difficult to determine which is the most appropriate answer. The respondents then tabulate their scores and the numerical values will correspond to one of the nine Enneagram types (Riso & Hudson, 2003; Schreiber & Shannon, 2001). The nine personality types are: The Reformer (rational, idealistic, and principled), the Helper (caring, interpersonal, and demonstrative), the Achiever (success-oriented, adaptive), the Individualist (sensitive, withdrawn, expressive), the Investigator (intense, cerebral, perceptive), the Loyalist (committed, security-oriented, engaging), the Enthusiast (busy, fun-loving, spontaneous), the Challenger (powerful, dominating, self-confident), and the Peace Maker (easygoing, self-effacing) (Matise, 2007; Riso & Hudson, 2003).

Kouzes and Posner's LPI

After Kouzes and Posner (2002) conducted their abovementioned original research, they developed the Leadership Practices Inventory (LPI) and have made it available to all who wish to reflect on and identify their leadership skills. The LPI provides information about leadership behavior and does not measure one's personality as does the Myers-Briggs Trait Indicator (Myers, 1998). The LPI has 30 questions that describe the gamut of leadership skills, and participants determine how frequently they exhibit these behaviors. Participants are required to answer all 30 questions using a Likert scale with responses ranging from Almost Never (1) to Almost Always (10). Kouzes and Posner indicate that all of the statements describe leadership activities based on their original research, and if the participant does not recognize one of the statements as reflecting leadership, the participant must not engage in this activity too often. Each item in the LPI addresses the patterns of best practices. The higher numerical value the respondent scores, the more closely aligned the respondent's skills are with the Five Practices of Exemplary Leadership (Kouzes & Posner, 2002).

In addition to the 30-question LPI, participants are to ask a few of their colleagues (manager, direct reporting supervisor, or coworker) to identify how well the participant engages in the behaviors described in the LPI from their perspective of being a colleague. This process of responding to the statements on the LPI, and having a colleague rate the respondent on the LPI, gives an extensive picture of the participant's leadership skills. Interestingly, the completed LPI by the respondent and the completed LPI by the observer do not always match. This disconnect in the scores may happen for a variety of reasons: some of the observers may not work with the respondent face to face; some observers may not know the respondent as well as others; as a leader, the respondent may act differently in different situations; observers may have different expectations of the respondent and finally, the respondent and each observer may interpret the meaning of the terms used in the Likert scale differently. Qualitative terms, such as "fairly" and "usually" have different meanings to different people (Kouzes & Posner, 2002). Nevertheless, the feedback the respondents receive from their own responses and those of the observers will delineate the leadership skills the respondents have, and the respondents will then have data to use in improving their skills and setting new leadership goals for self-improvement. Kouzes and Posner emphasize, however, that regardless of the feedback, the respondent needs to have the desire to improve or the data from the LPI is meaningless.

These three self-assessment tools, the Myers-Briggs Type Indicatory (Myers & Myers, 1995), the Enneagram Framework (Riso and Hudson 2003), and the Leadership Practices Inventory (Kouzes & Posner, 2002), are reliable and valid tools that school librarians may employ to learn and reflect on their personality types and their current leadership skills. Leaders improve their leadership skills only through self-reflection, knowledge, and desire.

SCHOOL LIBRARIANS' LEADERSHIP ROLES

School librarians should use this information to assess their own leadership qualities and learn more about their personalities through the self-assessment tools explained earlier. School librarians must be leaders and definitely leaders in the curriculum area. *Information Power: Guidelines for School Library Media Program* (AASL & AECT, 1988), *Information Power Building Partnerships for Learning* (AASL & AECT, 1998), and *Empowering Learners: Guidelines for*

School Library Programs (AASL, 2009) all analyze and discuss the school librarians' leadership roles. In these three organizing documents, school librarians are: information specialists, teachers, instructional consultants or instructional partners, program administrators, and leaders. All of these roles relate to the content curriculum of the classroom, the research inquiry curriculum in the school library, and the entire organization of the physical or virtual space where students and other members of the learning community have access to what they need to find, access, create, and evaluate information. As school librarians, our responsibility is to fulfill these roles; to do so, we must be leaders in our field.

WHAT DOES ALL OF THIS MEAN?

This chapter has presented introductory information about the concept of leadership. Leadership has many different definitions, and a plethora of leadership frameworks and theories abound. School librarians should determine what model resonates with their learning style and then implement that type of theory into their daily lives. School librarians should also reflect on their individual personality styles as self-knowledge will provide clues as to how they should develop as leaders. The leadership roles of school librarians were also identified so that school librarians understand their leadership responsibilities.

Reflective Questions

Reflect on the statement: Leaders are born not made.

Which of the leadership philosophies described in this chapter do you believe are relevant to your role as a leader in the school library, and why?

Which leadership theory could provide a leadership framework for you to follow?

Access one of the self-assessment inventories: Myers-Briggs, Enneagram or LPI; complete the self-assessment. What did you learn about yourself as a leader?

Chapter 3

School Culture and School Relationships

At the conclusion of this chapter, the reader will better understand the concept of a school as an organization and how the school's culture influences establishing a vibrant school library program. The reader will be able to assess the culture of a school and explore methods of establishing a positive school culture.

Jan had recently finished her college degree and was applying for a position as a high school social studies teacher. She was fortunate enough to have three or four interviews at different schools. Each of these interviews had different formats and requirements and told Jan about the school and its culture. When Jan arrived at one school 15 minutes early, the school representative asked her if she would like coffee, tea, or water and explained that the principal and the interview team would be available in a short time as they were just completing the previous interview. At another school Jan arrived and waited in the hallway as there was no one in the office. Finally, a school representative arrived and showed Jan the room for the interviews. At a third school, Jan had to wait by the front door for someone to arrive as the school was locked.

These differences continued during the interviews. At one school, the interview team consisted of the school principal and representatives from various departments in the school. The entire team shared in asking Jan questions and appeared to be very interested in her background, her education, and her goals as an educator. At another school, the principal asked all of the questions and the members of the interview team took notes during the interview. At the third school, the principal, alone, conducted the interview.

What Jan experienced during these interviews was a taste of the culture of each school. Each school handled the interviews differently from Jan's arrival to the conclusion of the interview. Each of the above scenarios illustrates the school's values and how business is handled. The scenarios are neither right nor wrong; they are simply a picture of how business is conducted in that organization.

As school librarians begin their positions at specific schools, they must be aware of the culture of the school to implement a successful school library program. Culture is a complex issue and can be examined by many different methods. Culture is an ingredient of the entire school that must be accounted for in establishing a twenty-first century library program.

Hartzell (1994) explains that schools are organizations in the same sense as medical facilities, businesses, and government entities. To analyze the culture of schools, the reader must have a basic knowledge of organizations and how they operate.

WHAT IS AN ORGANIZATION?

Many organizational theories have been developed since the early 1900s (Hatch, 1997). Hatch identifies five elements that influence the study of organizations: social structure, physical structure, culture, technology, and the environment. Various organizational theories have developed around each of these five strands (Argyris & Schon, 1978; DuFour & Eaker, 1998; Geertz, 1973; Hofstede & Hofstede, 2005; McGregor, 1985; Morgan, 1997; Peters & Waterman, 2004; Senge, 1990; Smirich, 1983). Each theory provides a method of scrutinizing the organization through its component parts.

One popular method of analyzing an entity is conceptualizing it as a learning organization (Henri, 2005; Copeland, 2003; Stolp, 1994). Senge (1990) describes a learning organization as one where the members are able to create the vision they desire, have their ideas nurtured, aspire to great heights, and continually learn. The organization becomes a learning organization when these component parts are present and the entity is analyzed as a whole package. This concept is based on von Buttetalanffy's General Systems Theory (Hatch, 1997), which acknowledges that organizations are comprised of many parts, but the essence of the system is visible only when it is analyzed as a whole. In his book, *The Fifth Discipline: The Art and Practice of the Leaning Organization* (1990), Senge uses the metaphor of a mirror to describe the learning organization. If one looks in a mirror, the reflection is a smooth image of oneself. If the mirror is shattered and the many pieces are glued back together, it is still one mirror, but the reflection is not a smooth image but one of many jagged parts and pieces. This distorted reflection awaits any leader who looks at the component parts of an organization without considering the organization as a whole. Principals must consider the entire school to move the program forward. Likewise, school librarians must analyze the entire school as a system to move the library program forward.

Senge (1990) identifies five component parts, or disciplines, that comprise an organization: *Systems Thinking; Personal Mastery; Mental Models; Building Shared Vision;* and *Team Learning.* These five parts need to be considered to see the true picture of the organization. *Systems Thinking* supports Senge's metaphor of the mirror. It is necessary to consider the entire organization to understand the organization fully. Looking at the accomplishments or deficits of only one part of the school will provide a skewed view of the organization as a whole. The concept of *Personal Mastery* is important as organizations consist of individuals, and unless each individual has a personal vision and set of goals, the individual will fail to continue to improve and develop. *Mental Models* are mental images that people have formed over their lifetimes based on their own personal experiences. They allow individuals to make snap decisions about other people or events they are witnessing. For example, if two people arrive at an event, one dressed in a professional suit with matching accessories, and one dressed in ragged blue jeans, T-shirt, and leather jacket, certain assumptions are made about these two individuals. These assumptions will be different for all of the people at the event, based on their previous experiences. These snap decisions based on our own experiences illustrate Senge's *Mental Model* and reflect a person's reality based on previous life experiences. They must be discussed openly and honestly when analyzing a person's role in the organization. The fourth component part of a learning organization is *Building a Shared Vision*. To move the organization forward, all members must be on the same page and dedicated to the same goals and vision. Without a shared vision, workers will simply be performing a job instead of supporting the culture of the organization. *Team Learning* is the final discipline that Senge develops. Members of the organization must create a shared history with each other as they move the organization forward. They must work together as a group, learn together as a group, and prosper together. This can be accomplished through team learning establishing a shared history.

But what does this theory have to do with school culture? Senge's (1990) means of analyzing an organization through these five disciplines provides us with a blueprint for looking at schools. As we analyze schools, we will also be studying a school's culture. A school is an organization with many departments, different functions, and various configurations. Schools must be considered as a total system as all the component parts are dependent on each other. The administrators, teachers, support staff, school librarian, other members of the learning community and their functions must be perceived as one system, one unit with a shared vision, a staff dedicated to individual personal mastery, a willingness to share ingrained mental models, and working together as a team, or school improvement and change will not occur. The culture will not improve.

WHAT IS CULTURE?

Debbie, a high school teacher, taught in one high school for five years. She shared that those were the best five years of her teaching career. When asked why, she wasn't sure how to answer the question. It was a combination of things: faculty, staff, students, location, and culture of the school. She indicated that every day when she arrived, she could feel an energy pulsating from the school. This energy was pulling her in. She knew that she was a member of something special and that by being pulled into the school, she would be able to implement the school's vision and accomplish her own professional goals.

Feeling the energy of being part of something great describes school culture. Although that is not a solid definition of the term *culture*, it is sometimes described that way. Many authors have written about school culture and have provided unique definitions of the concept (Bart, 2007; Deal & Peterson, 2009; Hallinger & Leithwood, 1998; Hargreaves, 1995; Kruse & Louis, 2009; Maehr & Midgley, 1996; Marzano, Waters, & McNulty, 2005; Peterson & Deal 1998; Purkey & Smith, 1982; Zmuda, Kuklis, & Kline, 2004). This is a partial list of authors addressing the issue, but it does provide an overview of culture that describes a school in detail. One workable formal definition is that culture is a collection of norms, values, beliefs, and traditions that emanate when teachers and administrators work together to solve problems, implement change, and confront challenges (Deal & Peterson, 2009). Bart (2007) simply states that culture is the way we do things around here. The energy Debbie experienced as she entered the doors to the school pointed to the culture of the school, and indicated that Debbie is a vital part of the school's culture. She has found a place, an organization where she fits. She is a productive member of the learning community and dedicates her efforts to assisting other teachers in how to affect student learning.

To learn more about a specific organization, culture must be considered. Schein (1992) exhorts leaders to examine culture for the following reasons:

1. By looking at culture, one can determine the subcultures that exist;
2. Analyzing culture will provide information on the role of technology and its influence on the organization;
3. Looking at culture supports the tenets of management across national and ethnic boundaries;
4. Change cannot be affected without understanding the prevailing culture may be resistant to change.

School librarians must consider the culture of the organization when establishing their library programs.

HOW DO WE MEASURE SCHOOL CULTURE?

Examining the existing culture to change it for the better is, indeed, important, but can this be done? Researchers have offered various methods to consider when analyzing culture (Deal & Peterson, 2009; Kruse & Lewis, 2009; Maehr & Midgley, 1996; Schein, 1992, 2010). Schein (1992, 2010) presents a tiered process of examining three distinct areas to understand and measure the culture of an organization: assumptions, values, and artifacts. Each of these levels when examined will offer an in-depth view of the culture of the organization, and each level provides a deeper understanding of the school as an organization.

The most difficult level of Schein's (1992) theory to understand is the level of assumptions. Assumptions are beliefs that people have about reality. They are the ideas that people know to be true based on their own life experiences. Sometimes these ideas are so deeply engrained in a people's psyche that they do not even realize they have this belief because it is so much a part of their makeup. Examples of these assumptions include religious beliefs, political views, ideas about the ways to achieve a happy life, and any ingrained idea or practice that makes each person unique. Assumptions are not easily changed as they are so much a part of a person. When two or more people get together, they each bring these innate beliefs with them. If they wish to form a group, faculty, or team, they must be aware of their own personal assumptions and mesh them with the assumptions of every person in the group.

Political beliefs are often at the assumption level. For example, some entire families have been members of the Democratic Party and would never consider joining another political party. When voting, they will vote a straight Democratic ballot, as this is part of their belief system. When a person with this innate belief meets a person who has the same views about the Republican Party, they must work together to modify their assumptions to collaborate with each other successfully. They must find a common ground.

Schein's (1992) second level of determining culture is through the values of the members of the organization. Values are not as innate as assumptions, and people are more conscious of their own values that are formed through their life experiences. As faculties and groups are formed in a school, members share their beliefs and the group accepts or modifies these values. The beliefs the members of the group embrace become new shared values and these shared values will be the catalyst for changing the values in the school.

An example should make this clearer. A new sixth-grade middle school team is formed. As the teachers meet, they realize they all have different ideas of how to implement classroom management. Rob's experiences have shown him that students respond to him better if he is easygoing rather than if he is an ogre. Karen, who is very shy, has had problems with classroom management and realizes that she needs to be strict to maintain control. Jill likes to be fairly relaxed with the students but has high standards the students need to reach. These three teachers will be working with each other, and their six-graders will have each of them as instructors at different times during the day. How will the group be effective when each member comes from three different ways of looking at and implementing classroom management? Schein (2010) argues that each of these teachers must discuss their styles of classroom management and determine a process that will reflect all of these management styles. As the teachers accomplish this, they have a new set of values based on their own innate beliefs that work for them.

Artifacts of an organization, Schein's (1992) third measurement of culture, are easy to identify. These representations give insight to the visible items that are important to the faculty and staff, and show how the school operates. Artifacts are traditions, ceremonies, and rituals that are predominant in a certain school. They tell the story of the school and what is important to the people who are part of the organization. Artifacts could be displays of student work, celebratory messages highlighting students who won contests supported by the school, or perhaps signs posted that celebrate students' heritage. Other signs that indicate what the teachers and staff support, such as procedures for keeping the school clean and looking nice, are artifacts that show what is important to the school. Artifacts are an easy way to understand the important details of school life.

This process of looking at artifacts, determining values, and analyzing assumptions is a method of determining the culture of an organization. Following Schein's (1992) process for determining culture provides a deep understanding of the culture of an organization. Appreciating this process makes us more aware of the school, its vision, its mission, and its values.

Determining the artifacts, values, and assumptions of an organization can be challenging. It is easy to identify artifacts as they are visual representations of procedures that are important to the school. As people join together and collaborate, their own personal values become evident, and the members can then discuss and reevaluate the values of the group. Assumptions are more difficult to determine, but they can become clearer with intense conversations and collaborations in safe environments. It is only by examining all three levels that we can develop an integrated belief system that will affect change in the school's culture. Many times, especially with assumptions and values, the lines are blurred as to where information should be placed: assumptions or values. Schein's theory provides for free-flowing movement among the three levels.

DETERMINING THE CULTURE OF AN INSTITUTION

Debbie, the high school teacher mentioned earlier, uses her intuition and emotions to describe the culture or the energy radiating from the school. Using personal perceptions is one way to begin studying the culture of an organization. The analysis of culture begins with the first encounter a person has with the institution or with members of the institution. Using Schein's (1992) method, the observer should first be aware of the artifacts in the institution; then look at the values of the teachers, administrators, and staff, and then try to determine the assumptions of individual members of the faculty or the shared assumptions they have.

The first encounter with the school may be through an interview for a position. Applicants need to be well prepared to answer the individual questions posed them, but they must also analyze the climate of the school and the attitude of the members of the interview team. It is important to evaluate the interview process. How comfortable was the climate in the room? Did the members of the interview team seem to like each other? How did they interact with the principal? What was their body language? Did they show displeasure about anything in any way? In other words, did they roll their eyes when you or others were speaking? Did they frown when others were talking? Were they sitting there comfortably or did their bodies scream "stress"? When you are asked if you have any questions, watch the members of the team. Did they seem nervous by the question you asked? Did they give you the impression that your question was a silly one to ask? Who answered your question? Was it the principal or was it one of the members of the team? Did you ascertain that the principal was a driving force in the school or was very controlling? An interview happens quickly and the applicant may not be able to determine what the culture is really like until the applicant is offered a job. When applying for positions, the applicants must be aware of the culture as much as possible.

Now the person is hired. This presents a better opportunity to understand the culture of the school as an employee. During the first few weeks of school the new employee should continue this analysis of the culture and climate of the school. Schein's (1992) system provides a road map to acquire the needed information. The following list gives examples of questions that can be used to determine the existing culture of an organization using artifacts, values, and assumptions.

Artifacts:

What items are displayed in the hallways and in the classrooms?

Are there student papers hanging throughout the school?

Are the activities of each classroom displayed in the main hallway or by the classrooms?

What items are covered in the announcements?

Are they items that students will find interesting?

Are the announcements used every day?

Do the announcements celebrate the students in the classrooms as members of the school?

Values:

Do the teachers seem friendly?

Do they give emotional support to each other?

Do they seem to like each other?

How do they interact with each other?

How do they get along with the principal?

Is the principal respected?

Do the teachers respect and value the office staff?

How is the office staff treated?

Are they made to feel special all of the time or just during secretary's week?

Assumptions:

Do the teachers and staff have the same interests that you do?

Do they really mean that they want students to succeed?

What evidence do you have that the teachers support success for each child?

What types of activities do the teachers support?

What are the activities before and after school?

What are the school clubs?

How are athletic and extracurricular activities supported?

Do the teachers support the students in these endeavors?

These questions are only a few that can be asked and the answers reflected on as members of a school are trying to learn more about the school and its culture. New members of the staff can use these questions, but it is also productive to systematically analyze the culture of a school periodically to make certain the administrators, faculty, and staff are all working together to increase student learning.

HOW CAN ONE CHANGE THE CULTURE OF THE SCHOOL?

Schein's (1992) method allows us to determine the culture of a specific organization. One must work with the administrators, teachers, and staff to make positive improvements to the school's culture. When a district is preparing to build a new school, establishing a positive direction for this culture is an established process. Various methods of planning and organizing for a new school can be used. The following steps should be considered when embarking on this venture. The principal and administrative staff are identified many months prior to the opening of the school in order for them to work with the contractors through every facet of the construction. One of the most important responsibilities that will guide the school for years to come is the hiring of teachers and staff members. Selecting these individuals will establish the culture of the school. To hire the appropriate teachers and staff, the administrators need to know and understand their personal vision of the school and the vision of the school district. With each new selection, the administrators will discuss and explain the nucleus of the vision that will guide the school. As each new person is added to the team, the vision will be refocused and solidified incorporating the assumptions and values of the new team members. The slate is blank and through the nucleus of the vision and the ideas of the teachers and staff, something new is born. There will be very few if any people standing in the way of developing this shared vision of the administrators, teachers, and staff as this is a new organization. One of the crucial hires in this new team is the school librarian. The school librarian needs to help shape this new vision as the school moves forward. Being a member of the core team allows the school librarian to align the vision of the school library program with the school's vision. The vision of the classroom teachers, administrators, and the school librarian will meld together.

Being on the core team when a new school is established does not occur very often and some educators never have this experience. In general, becoming a member of a school occurs by filling a vacancy and joining an organization that has an established culture that permeates the entire community: administrators, teachers, staff members, students, and members of the learning community. This challenge is one faced by most school librarians.

Joyce was hired at Stoddard Elementary School. As she arrived on her first day, she was excited about the challenges that lay before her. She understands that she must determine what the culture of Stoddard is and how it is conducive to establishing an effective school library program. Her personal vision is to work with every student, staff, and member of the learning community to provide a physical space and a virtual reality of promoting learning and assisting students in finding, evaluating, accessing, and creating the information they need in their everyday lives. This vision aligns with the vision of the school. As the days rush by, Joyce understands that although her vision and the school's vision align, the culture of the school displays another set of values. The teachers arrive a few minutes before their classes and leave the building as soon as the final dismissal bell rings. The teachers send the students to the library but do not work with Joyce to collaborate on any lessons. The teachers expect Joyce to be at their beck and call for any needs they may have, whether it be a problem with a computer or copying an assignment they need for class. All of the teachers are traveling their own path and never stray from the course that will inconvenience them in any way. Joyce sees the culture as one that is teacher-centered and that satisfying the needs of the teachers is a paramount duty and responsibility of the support staff and the school librarian.

Joyce could become depressed with this situation if she would let herself. Instead she decides to change this toxic culture and move the faculty, staff, and principal back to the original vision of the school. Joyce must consider the two following items when changing the culture.

Interpersonal Relationships

Organizations are made up of people and the people decide the culture of the organization. The school librarian should make a concentrated effort to meet each member of the instructional and administrative staff. This meeting is more than an introduction because new faculty members are formally intro-duced at the first faculty meeting. The purpose of these individual meetings is to determine if the school librarian has any connections with individual members of the staff. Do they have any common likes and dislikes? Do they read the same authors or like the same types of books? Do they have the same hobbies? Do they like the same types of food or music or computers? As these meetings take place, the school librarian will determine what common grounds they have and how their common interests can be developed. These meetings are informal and usually take place during lunch time, or during the faculty members' planning periods. These are not formal encounters but rather informal conversations where the school librarian is able to learn more about the members of the school community. School librarians must show their likes and dislikes, so the faculty will begin to know them better. The school librarian is seen as a friendly person who likes people and works hard to know all of the students and the staff.

Role of Influence in Interpersonal Relationships

As Joyce learns about the members of the faculty and their backgrounds, she must be aware of the existing influence that faculty members have with the principal, the other faculty members, and with members of the learning com-munity. Hartzell (1994) exhorts the school librarian to be aware of the influence that different members of the faculty have and to understand how the school librarians must develop their own sphere of influence. As school librarians begin to know the teachers and staff members, they should be aware of the per-ceptions that the faculty have of the school library program. If the school librar-ian has been trained to establish a collaborative culture through the library program and members of the faculty think the school library is a warehouse of resources, then the school librarian must take steps to change this perception. This change will occur gradually but can be changed. One way to affect this change is by developing trust.

Developing Trust

The faculty must trust the school librarian. Trust is born through honesty in general encounters and in highly charged ones. The school librarian must show he or she is an honest person, a reliable one, and a person who can be counted on every day and during any crisis that may occur. Developing trust takes time and there is no easy formula for this. Trust is developed through myriad interactions as two people get to know each other and begin respecting each other and their individual views. Trust does not mean that two people have identical beliefs but it does mean that two people respect their differences and know that each person is honest with each other. If the school librarian is asked to complete a project, it will be completed. If the library is not available for one teacher's class because of a scheduling issue, it is not available to any other class for the same reason. The school librarian is reliable and fair to all members of the learning community.

The key concept is "baby steps." As Joyce tries to change the culture, she must do so by taking baby steps and celebrating her successes however small. It may take three to five years to establish an effective library program, but she can start the first day she arrives at the school. Establishing trust and building interpersonal relationships take time and must be accomplished gradually.

WHAT DOES ALL OF THIS MEAN?

This chapter examined the concept of culture. What is it and how can it be measured? Why is it important? Some authors talk about the climate of the school or the environment. All three words address the same issue. Each organization, each school has a certain atmosphere. School librarians need to identify whether the culture is one supporting learning or one that is toxic. Then they need to determine how to best work within the culture of that school, supporting the positive aspects of the culture and changing the negative aspects. School librarians must work with their colleagues to improve the culture of the school, and this can be accomplished through building interpersonal relationships.

Reflective Questions

What type of culture have you found in a school or organization where you have been employed?

What other steps would you encourage Joyce to take to change the culture of her school?

Think of your experience in high school, college, or for a post graduate degree. How would you describe the culture of that institution?

Think of this same institution and use Schein's (1992) method to determine the assumptions, values, and artifacts of the organization.

What is the first step you will take to understand the culture of your school?

Chapter 4

Curriculum Mapping

After reading this chapter, the school librarian will understand the concept of curriculum mapping, the process of creating a curriculum map, and be introduced to some of the challenges of developing a curriculum map. The school librarian will understand the value of using this tool when working with the teachers in the school.

Long, long ago in a city far, far away, high school librarian Donna was working with a ninth-grade speech teacher who had assigned her students a three-minute speech on current issues. Donna and the teacher were strategizing on what resources the students could use, how many days they should book space and time in the library, and what roles the teacher and the school librarian would play. The next day the ninth-grade history teacher approached Donna and described a lesson where his students would conduct research on a current topic in preparation for a three-minute speech project. Unfortunately, both of these excellent teachers were caught up in the isolation that is inherent in the lives of classroom teachers (Hartzell, 1994) as neither one realized the other teacher was assigning a similar project. The school librarian is in a unique position of understanding the big picture of curriculum being taught in the school. The school librarian can be the linchpin that unites the spokes in the wheel of the curriculum. One tool that can be used to help with this leadership role is curriculum mapping.

In Chapter 1, What Is Curriculum, we discussed the different parameters of this word and its implications for school districts. We also learned that curriculum is driven by content standards, research inquiry standards, and technology standards. Looking at curriculum and the standards movement globally, states have aligned their curriculum with these standards, districts have developed frameworks to implement these standards, schools have interpreted the district framework, grade level collaborative groups have implemented this framework, and finally, individual teachers have worked with the students in their classrooms to increase student learning (see Table 4.1). As each of these levels completes the implementation and interpretation of this standards-based curriculum, changes may inadvertently occur. By the time this curriculum reaches the classroom teacher, the classroom lessons may not reflect the

Table 4.1 Levels of Curriculum Implementation

Levels of Curriculum Implementation	
Level 1	State
Level 2	District Framework
Level 3	School Interpretation
Level 4	Grade Level Implementation
Level 5	Individual Classroom

initial curriculum mandate. It may be difficult to determine who is teaching what, when it is being taught, and how the material is being presented. Because American History is taught at two different grade levels, how can educators make certain students are seeing the whole spectrum of history and not repeating the same material during both classes? Curriculum mapping is a tool that can be used to learn what is being taught at which level and addressing which content, research inquiry, and technology standards. This tool will enable school librarians to exercise their leadership role as instructional partners

WHAT IS CURRICULUM MAPPING?

Curriculum mapping is a tool used to determine what is being taught when and how in an educational institution. It provides a visual image of what curriculum is being presented in each classroom during each year (Jacobs, 1997). The detailed curriculum map illustrates the essential question, the standards, the skills, the activities, and the assessments that instructors present to their students at specific times during the school year. From a curriculum map, the principal, the teachers including the school librarian, and the parents can see what their students are studying at any point during the year.

The concept of a curriculum map is simply that: a map. It illustrates how teachers and students will travel from Point A to Point B and what they will accomplish along the way. It clarifies the essential questions, the goals of the unit, the activities, the standards to be addressed, and the assessment of student learning. When school librarians have this information about each unit being taught in the school, they can work closely with different teachers and grade levels to enhance student learning.

School librarians are not always aware of what is being taught in the classrooms. On the surface, they should be able to gather this information from the lesson plans the classroom teachers have developed, but these documents may not always be available. In this case, the best way for school librarians to gather this information is to simply ask the teachers what they are presenting in their classes and then keep track of this information on a spreadsheet or similar document. Often, however, retrieving this information may be more difficult than it seems. For the school librarians to fulfill their roles as information specialists and to prepare to be an instructional partner, they must devise ways to gather this information. With this information, the school librarian can then create a curriculum map to illustrate the skills and content the students will study during the year.

BARRIERS: TEACHING IN ISOLATION

Why is it so hard for the school librarian to gather curriculum information? One reason is that teachers sometimes work in isolation (Hartzell, 1994; Udelhofen, 2005). They have their own classrooms, their own students, and the entire school day to create a learning environment for these students. This isolation creates an environment conducive to working with the students on what the teacher perceives as students' needs, on content that the teacher wants to share with the students, or addressing the mandated state or local standards. This scenario provides a situation in which the teachers believe they are following the required curriculum but may, in fact, be deviating from the standard curriculum framework. Some teachers may cover the required material as quickly as possible so that they are free to work with their students on content they feel is important or fun to teach. One such incident occurred some time ago, when a middle-school teacher covered the required curriculum as quickly as possible so that he could spend six weeks on the assassination of John F. Kennedy. This era of American history was part of the high school American history curriculum.

Although teachers create a warm, social atmosphere in their classrooms, many times the socialization stops there. Teachers' classrooms are their own little worlds and they are often unaware of what is happening with other colleagues in the school. The arrangement of classrooms in the school supports this isolation and makes interacting with other teachers sometimes difficult (Cookson, 2005). Classrooms are arranged in hallways, usually with fixed walls and a confined space, neatly configured for teachers to work with their students. The lockstep schedule supports this isolation as teachers work to provide for the needs of each of their students.

This isolated condition in these learning environments addresses the immediate needs of the students but clouds the process of the educational journey that each student travels. In recent years, the idea of integrating content across classrooms helps mitigate teacher isolation but more work needs to be accomplished in this area. Integrating class content allows teachers to work together in different configurations with a variety of content areas. Elementary schools have grade-level teams who meet frequently to deliver the curriculum to their assigned students. Middle schools are often arranged in core groups, sometimes called houses or teams, where the instructors work only with the students in that group. High schools still tend to have individual classrooms, but some have moved toward core groups similar to middle school configurations. Some schools have implemented Professional Learning Communities (PLC) based on the work of DuFour and Eaker (1998) and Hall and Hord (2006). Using PLCs and other collaborative groups helps with breaking down the barrier of isolation that is inherent in the teaching profession. Chapter 8, Learning Community, will look more closely at these collaborative groups.

The library is the school librarian's classroom and isolation may also permeate this space. The isolation of the classroom teacher is a barrier that the

Table 4.2 Investigating Classroom Content

Ask a teacher.
Ask the teachers to complete a calendar of when units are taught during the semester.
Listen to students.
Visit classrooms when instruction is occurring.
Have casual conversations with individual teachers.

school librarian must overcome. The collaborative nature of the school librarian's role requires him or her to work with all of the teachers in the school. School librarians need to know the curriculum content being presented in the classrooms to help eliminate this sense of isolation.

How can this isolation be overcome? There are various ways the school librarian can begin breaking down the barrier of this isolation. One simple approach is to ask teachers what units are being presented during the semester. Some teachers will readily share this information. School librarians may want to create a calendar form the teachers could complete, indicating the units that are offered at their grade levels each month of the semester. One positive way is to listen to the students as they visit the library. As school librarians are working with the students on their research assignments, and by asking clarifying questions, they will gather some of the needed information. Some school librarians like to visit classrooms to learn more about the curriculum and the teachers. If they decide to visit specific classrooms, it is important to ask the teachers' permission. Some teachers will be fine with this and others will prefer that the school librarian does not come into their classrooms. Another strategy to use is having casual conversations with the teachers. These informal interactions can occur on the fly through lunchtime conversations, in the library, or even during other assignments such as supervision duties. These informal conversations may be a valuable source of information for the school librarian who is trying to complete the curriculum maps. Regardless of how school librarians learn the topics being presented in the classroom, this information is crucial to constructing a curriculum map. Table 4.2 lists various methods school librarians can use to determine the curriculum being taught in the classrooms.

Teachers each have a classroom, a set group of students, and curriculum based on standards that need to be accomplished. As teachers present lessons to their students to achieve the stated objectives, they are constantly evaluating, adding new lessons to make their presentations more effective. If members of the faculty do collaborate on plans, individual teachers teaching fourth-graders in the same school may still be presenting completely different information. Curriculum mapping will determine where these differences occur.

WHAT IS THE PROCESS OF CURRICULUM MAPPING?

Jacobs (1997) describes the first step in curriculum mapping as collecting data. Teachers completing a curriculum map of the content they are teaching

Table 4.3   Classroom Curriculum Overview

Curriculum Overview Mr. Hunter, Eleventh-Grade American History 1900 to the Present		
Date	**Unit**	**Duration**
September	World War I	Three weeks
End of September through October 30th	World War II	Five weeks
November 1st through end of November	Korean War	3 weeks (Thanks-giving vacation)
December 1st through January 10th	Vietnam War	5 weeks (Winter break)

would begin by listing each unit taught during each month of the year. This does not need to be a complicated process, and the teacher would use a chart similar to the one seen in Table 4.3.

Table 4.3 gives an example of a form school librarians could use to ascertain the order and duration of the units being presented in the classroom. Mr. Hunter teaches high school juniors and covers the major conflicts occurring in American History from 1900 to the present. Based on the Curriculum Overview form, the school librarian has a good idea of how many weeks he will spend on each conflict during the first semester of a school year. Mr. Hunter would continue listing the units covered during the rest of the semester and a basic curriculum map would be completed. The Curriculum Overview form asks the teacher to provide only the basic information that opens the door for the school librarian to gather additional information through individual discussions. This process makes it easy for teachers and allows the school librarian to continue developing relationships with them. Additional information the school librarian could gather would be: essential questions for the unit, the standards addressed, the skills and processes presented, the unit activities, and the assessments developed to measure the students' progress. When all of the teachers complete a Curriculum Overview form, the school librarian will have a blueprint of all of the units being presented in the school for the entire year.

This process will be global for the school librarians, because they need to be aware of all the units being taught in all the grades in all the classrooms. Challenges may occur as the school librarian tries to obtain this information. Even though the Curriculum Overview is an easy form to complete, teachers may not complete it because of their busy schedules. Time is always a factor, and classroom teachers never seem to have enough time to accomplish all they need to. Even if the school librarian contacts each classroom teacher via e-mail, the e-mail may get lost in the teacher's mailbox pile of "to be answered later."

"Need" presents another challenge. Perhaps the classroom teachers do not see the need for the school librarian to have this information. The "need" reason is a complex topic that the school librarian must address. The school librarian is responsible for creating a cornucopia of sources that will provide students with the information they need to accomplish the curriculum framework. On a basic level, school librarians need to know which sources to order and in which formats to support students' learning. The second reason is more all-pervasive. School librarians see the entire curriculum, are familiar with each subject area and discipline, and understand the content and competencies that students should have as they travel on their paths to becoming educated. As instructional leaders, school librarians must assist in designing the pathways that students follow. Simply put, students should not repeatedly study the same topics each time they are exposed to literary works; rather, they should see the broad spectrum of all types of work without multiple duplications. Studying the same novel at two different grade levels is repetitious and should not occur. With the number of selections in literature at all grade levels, students should not study the same novel more than one time. The school librarian has a perfect vantage point to make certain that students are not repeating curriculum.

The challenges of "need" and "time" should be addressed, and the school librarian may need to use other strategies to gather this information from the classroom teachers (see Table 4.2). By gathering this information from each teacher on the faculty, the school librarian then has the first phase of the curriculum map completed.

As school librarians collect these data through interactions with the teachers, they should compile the data using a spreadsheet or a chart. The spreadsheet reflects the information the school librarians have collected from each of the teachers, including a column identifying any further comments, questions, or follow-up notes. After the master chart is completed, the school librarian will have a better overview of the curriculum and what is being taught. This process may be lengthy. In high schools, for example, many courses are completed in a semester, which means the data may be collected during that semester. However, in elementary schools and some middle schools, it may take up to a year to rotate through the entire curriculum projects. Therefore, school librarians must be patient and persistent in their quest for the information.

As school librarians gather this information from classroom teachers and students, they should compare these data with the school district's curriculum framework and the textbooks being used in the classes. Any gaps or omissions noted between the teacher data and the framework should be shared with the faculty at an appropriate time. After the school librarians have completed this overview of the curriculum, they should share this information with the principal, members of the leadership teams, and individual teachers. Rich discussions will follow as the stakeholders see the blueprint of the curriculum. This information is an overview only and the faculty and school librarian must look at the information through both a horizontal and vertical lens.

HORIZONTAL LENS-HORIZONTAL MAPPING

The next step in curriculum mapping is to look at each grade level or each section of the same class and compare the information found on the Curriculum

Overview form or the master spreadsheet. The following questions are typical and could be asked of a group of third-grade teachers working with science:

- Are all of the third-grade teachers presenting the same content to the students?
- If "bugs" is the science topic for the first semester, are all of the third-grade students receiving instruction concerning "bugs"?
- Which science standards address "bugs"?
- Are all of the third-grade teachers addressing these same standards?
- What types of projects are the third-graders expected to complete in this unit?
- Are all of the third-graders performing or completing these units?
- Which assessment tool does each teacher use to measure a student's progress?
- Is the assessment tool the same or similar for each student regardless of the classroom teacher? Does the assessment tool measure a student's required progress?
- If Johnny transfers from Ms. Jones's science class to Mr. Smith's science class, will the content be the same?
- Will Johnny have the same learning experience in Mr. Smith's class as he did in Ms. Jones's class?

This process of looking at the student experience through the grade-level lens is called horizontal curriculum mapping. A few years ago, when working with a group of eighth-grade middle school English teachers at the same school who were comparing notes on what they were presenting to the students, one teacher said, "I love teaching research but I hate grading the research paper." Another teacher said, "What paper? I just have the students conduct the research as we never have time for the paper itself." And yet another said, "I have them do a five-paragraph essay as they are familiar with that so it doesn't take so much time."

With three separate answers from three individual teachers each of whom were teaching the same class in the same middle school, it is interesting that the teachers were surprised by the differences in the final assignment and that the assignments were all different. Which assignment is the one that should be used? It depends. There is not a right or wrong answer. The teachers need to decide what is best for the students and then reflect that on the school's curriculum framework. All of the eighth-grade teachers need to be involved in this discussion. Each eighth-grader in this middle school should have the same academic experience, be it a five-paragraph essay, an exercise in research, or an entire research paper.

Achieving consensus from all of the teachers at a specific grade level or high school content specialists teaching the same class could be challenging. The school librarian will need to work with the teachers to determine as a group what they believe is the best for the students and what needs to be accomplished. This overall school-wide process will require the support of the principal and the commitment of the classroom teachers including the department chairs. School librarians will be involved in these conversations and need to show their leadership skills throughout the entire process. The school-wide curriculum mapping process will be discussed later in this chapter.

The school librarian should begin this process on a smaller scale by working with the teachers at the individual grade levels or content areas to see if a consensus can be reached among the teachers. This process would include reviewing the curriculum maps from each teacher and comparing the essential questions, activities, and assessments that each teacher uses. These rich discussions will set the teams on a trajectory to plan and organize the curriculum for the students at this grade level or in a specific content area. The goal of these meetings will be to align what each individual teacher is accomplishing in the individual classroom and to align the overall content with the school's curriculum framework, the district's curriculum framework, and state and national standards.

VERTICAL LENS-VERTICAL MAPPING

After consensus is reached at each level through a horizontal lens, the curriculum should be evaluated through a vertical lens. The process of vertical mapping is a school-wide process as the concepts presented at one level are then aligned with the concepts presented at all levels. Looking back at the elementary concept of "bugs" that was mentioned earlier, the third-grade teachers would now need to hone in on the standards, essential questions, activities, and skills associated with "bugs." The teachers need to ask the following questions:

- Are "bugs" being studied at any other grade level?
- Is any other grade level addressing the same standards?
- Is any other grade level using the same essential questions?
- Are the skills and activities we are presenting also being studied at another level?
- Are the assessment tools we are using appropriate, or is there a duplication at another grade level?

The answers to these questions will be crucial to understand the educational journey students take to complete their studies. This assessment through vertical mapping can be summarized by a conversation that teachers often have at all levels. It usually occurs when teachers discuss novels to be presented to children. "You can't use *The Hunger Games* (Collins, 2008) at the seventh-grade level; we use it at the eighth-grade level." When I was a school librarian at a high school, I remember the many discussions we had as to which class—freshmen or juniors—could study Shakespeare's *Romeo and Juliet* (1964). Sometimes teachers, unable to reach consensus, decide to use the play at both levels, rationalizing that if the students use the book as freshmen and again as seniors, they will study the work more in-depth. This idea could be true; but the fact remains that if the curriculum is mapped according to essential questions, content, and assessment exercises, a duplication of resources would not be

Table 4.4 Process of Horizontal and Vertical Curriculum Mapping

Horizontal Lens	Vertical Lens
— Determine what is being taught in each classroom in the school using a Curriculum Overview form or other method. — Follow up with individual discussions to gather additional data including essential questions, standards, activities, and other information. — Create a master spreadsheet with the data. — Share data with principal and leadership team when appropriate. — Meet individually with each grade level comparing the overviews of each teacher. — Identify differences and reach consensus on how to align curriculum overviews.	— After reviewing the grade level information, work with specific grade levels to compare the data from all of the other grade levels. — Determine if there is duplication in what is being offered at different grade levels. — Compare data with the school curriculum framework and the district curriculum framework. — Reach consensus on any duplications. — Revise curriculum as appropriate.

needed. In this day of a plethora of resources, there are almost too many choices as to the best source to use. It is unnecessary to repeat the use of a resource and it is not beneficial to the students. Vertical mapping allows the process of planning to unfold. It takes a commitment to the student and engagement by the teachers and the principal to make it work, but it is worth it. Collecting data on the success of the students will assist teachers in determining which resource to use at which level.

Horizontal and vertical mapping are both necessary for the principal, the school librarian, and the teachers to map the student's educational journey. Each process focuses on different configurations of data the teachers can provide. The school librarian needs to be familiar with the process of both horizontal and vertical mapping to create a complete picture of how the curriculum is being presented to the students. Table 4.4 gives a good overview of each process.

THE SCHOOL LIBRARIAN'S ROLE

In this chapter we have examined the school librarian's role in assisting with horizontal and vertical curriculum mapping. This knowledge is crucial for school librarians in developing the collection maps, which is the subject of Chapter 5. The school librarians must also be involved with curriculum mapping to determine how they will implement the school library curriculum. Where will the information literacy, media literacy, visual literacy, and technology literacy standards be addressed? How will the students learn the inquiry research model? AASL (2009), in *Empowering Learners: Guidelines for School Library Programs*, identifies the school librarian's curriculum role in the educational process. As school librarians begin to understand the vertical and horizontal mapping of the curriculum for their schools, they should also project where the school library standards will be infused into the curriculum. School librarians should work with the teachers to develop a cohesive and comprehensive plan to implement an inquiry process for each of the students at each grade level. This concept of infusing the school library curriculum into the existing classroom curriculum will be addressed further in Chapter 7, Instructional Partner and Change. School librarians are critical in this discussion as they know the resources available and what materials are needed for all of the grade levels to complete the same assignments and to provide the same educational experience for each of the students.

SCHOOL-WIDE CURRICULUM MAPPING

In this chapter we have looked at the school librarian's role in beginning the process of curriculum mapping to learn what the teachers are accomplishing in their classrooms. The school librarian needs this information to better understand how to work with the teachers and the students, how to implement the school library curriculum, and to begin determining what resources are needed for successful lessons to occur in the classroom. These processes will assist the school librarian in achieving the goal of curriculum mapping.

For curriculum mapping to be effective and used as a tool for curriculum review and design, it must become part of the entire school process. This now expands from the school librarian's initial efforts to the school-wide commitment of the entire faculty and staff. Some may wonder why this process of curriculum mapping is so important. If the school librarian needs this information to provide the resources necessary to work with the teachers and the students, that is fine. But why would it need to be done on a school-wide and even a district-wide scale?

Let's reflect for a minute. Are the students different today than they were 10 years ago? Of course they are. Will the jobs that the students hold when they leave the K-12 system be different than they were 10 years ago? Yes, they will. In fact, in educating students today, we are preparing them for jobs that may not now exist. Jacobs (2010) wonders if students entering our schools feel like they are traveling back to an age that has long since passed. They return to the current century only when they once again leave school for the day.

To prepare the students for the world they will enter after school, educators need to develop a curriculum that is relevant to the twenty-first century. This curriculum must include content standards, research and inquiry standards, new technologies, and new pedagogical activities. In other words, the current curriculum must be reviewed in light of today's world, and changes must be implemented. School-wide curriculum mapping is a tool that will assist in this process. The basic process of horizontal and vertical curriculum mapping stays the same, but engagement of the administrators and members of the leadership team will provide the impetus to create this culture of collaboration.

Udelhofen (2005) proposes that to reevaluate, develop, and change curriculum, students must be placed in the center of the discussion. The principal must establish a collaborative culture in the school and create an atmosphere of trust among faculty members. Given the isolation of the teaching profession, it is difficult to automatically open up and share the entire curriculum a teacher is presenting in an individual classroom. The principal and leadership team must also determine when and how teachers will have the time and tools to create their own curriculum maps and share them with other members of the faculty. The principal must be an agent of change to implement a school-wide curriculum mapping project.

What is the school librarian's role in this process? The school librarian began this process on a smaller scale. Now the school librarian must eagerly support the principal to infuse this process throughout the school.

WHAT DOES ALL OF THIS MEAN?

School librarians have been responsible for developing the collections in school libraries for many years. Today it is imperative that school librarians align the research and inquiry processes with the rest of the curriculum in the school. This chapter explained the process of curriculum mapping that is a useful tool in identifying the curriculum at each grade level, in each class at all levels in the K-12 arena. This tool is one that school librarians will use to better understand what the classroom teachers are presenting to the students and how the research and inquiry process will be infused into this curriculum. School librarians should start small with the classroom teachers and then, working with the leadership team, they will be able to implement curriculum planning throughout the school. The curriculum mapping process helps the school librarians fulfill their leadership role as information specialists and instructional partners.

Reflective Questions

What is the value of a curriculum map?

What is the difference between vertical mapping and horizontal mapping?

Why is it important to map vertically and horizontally?

What is the school librarian's role in a school-wide curriculum mapping effort?

How does the school librarian exhibit leadership skills in working with the administrator and faculty while developing a curriculum map?

Chapter 5

Collection Mapping

After reading this chapter, the school librarian will understand the concept of collection mapping and the process of creating a collection map, be made aware of the challenges in developing the map, and understand the relationship of the collection map to the curriculum maps and to collection development.

When a new school is built, the school district earmarks a certain number of funds to provide resources for the entire school population. Although these resources are spread throughout the school, a significant number of funds provide resources for the school library. School librarians resemble children in a candy store, selecting all the sweets they desire to satiate their appetites. School librarians with this type of opportunity know the parameters of the curriculum and the research and information needs of the students. Most of us are neither in the position of opening a new school nor do we have the luxury of purchasing a number of items for our students all at once. Most of us inherit collections that have some great items but also contain the old, sometimes ancient, copies of materials that need to be discarded. One tool to evaluate such an inherited collection is collection mapping.

WHAT IS A COLLECTION MAP?

Like a curriculum map, a collection map is a snapshot of what materials are available in a collection at a specific point in time (Howard, 2010b). Loertscher and Wimberley (2009) describe a collection map as a means for the librarian to know what is in the collection by looking at the collection divided into smaller parts. The first purpose of a collection map is to help the school librarian know what is in the collection (see Figure 5.1). To prepare collection maps, both qualitative and quantitative information is needed to assist the school librarian in understanding the component parts of the collection and the value of the collection to the library users. Another value of the collection map is to determine the strengths and weaknesses of the collection (Bishop, 2013). Collection maps

43

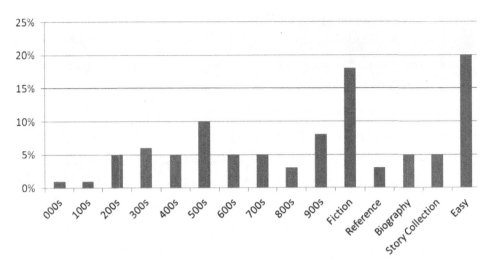

Figure 5.1   Collection Map

provide information about which books are old and outdated and should be weeded from the collection. This information can then be shared with decision makers when requesting additional budgetary funds. Collection maps are very valuable for this reason.

HOW DO I PREPARE A COLLECTION MAP?

To determine the contents of the collection, the school librarian should look at the collection globally. The inventory list provides an overall view of the resources. Before the explosion of the Internet, libraries kept track of their resources through a shelf list in the form of cards from the card catalog, or through a paper list of all of the resources. Today the majority of libraries are automated, so understanding the breadth of resources is much easier, quicker, and more efficient. Most automated systems can run a list of items in the catalog, indicating which item is checked out, when it was last checked out, if it is missing, or if it has been withdrawn from the collection. This list provides the data the school librarian needs to learn about the items in the collection. Vendors are now very helpful with running data reports providing a breakdown of the Dewey numbers or other classification system, including a total number of items for each section. These reports will indicate when the item was last checked out and the number of times it has circulated in the last few years. All of these data give the school librarian a pretty good sense of the items in the collection. This information will help the librarian determine how to proceed with the collection map. Before creating a collection map, the school librarian should reflect on a series of questions.

- How should I divide the collection?
- Which classification system should I use?
- Should I change the focus at this point?

- Do I look at each area and subgroup of the classification system (Dewey, LC, or other)?
- Do I consider all of the formats together or should I evaluate the print resources first and then consider the electronic resources?
- What do I do about "old" formats such as DVDs and CDs?

After these questions have been answered, the school librarian is ready to create the actual collection map. To create a collection map, the school librarian should follow these ten easy steps (Table 5.1).

Table 5.1   Steps in Collection Mapping

Step 1: Locating all of the resources.	Print, nonprint, electronic
Step 2: Determining how to divide the collection into smaller parts.	
Step 3: Decide which parts will be analyzed first.	Begin with the oldest or the one that needs to be reviewed immediately. If a new curriculum is being adopted, then this section of the collection should be evaluated prior to purchasing additional materials.
Step 4: Determine the number of items in this section.	Electronically through the Integrated Library System (ILS) or through the old-fashioned way of counting resources.
Step 5: Print a list of holdings and match the list with the items on the shelf.	Block off that part of the collection so that the School Librarian can evaluate the collection. Create a workflow to have items that are currently checked-out evaluated when they are returned to the library.
Step 6: Evaluate each item through quantitative measures.	
Step 7: Evaluate the physical condition of each item through qualitative measures.	
Step 8: Evaluate the content and relevance of each item through weeding guidelines.	
Step 9: Decide which items should be eliminated.	
Step 10: Reflect information on the Collection Map.	

STEP 1: LOCATE ALL OF THE MATERIALS IN THE COLLECTION

When a student walks into the school library or a patron walks into a public library, it may not be obvious what resources are available. This would be step one: locating all of the sources available, print, nonprint, and electronic. If the school library has a physical space, then the location of the books will be easy to determine. There may be additional book resources available in another area of the building, in the basement, or even possibly in a Quonset hut somewhere on the property. Although a Quonset hut may be unreasonable, the school librarian must be aware of all the locations where the resources are and make certain there isn't some out of the way storage area where materials have been stored. Another more realistic place to look is in the classroom collections.

- Are these materials on the library inventory?
- Are they not on the inventory but should be?
- Are they marked as missing?
- Do the items in the classroom libraries belong to the teachers' personal collections?
- Is this something the school librarian should include in the collection map because of the emphasis on curriculum standards?

All of these questions should be considered when the school librarian is trying to locate the resources that are part of the school library collection. Some of the questions are difficult to answer especially when the resources are not housed in the library proper.

The nonprint materials may be available in a separate room or area in the library and are easily accessible to the school librarian. There may be a professional collection that is housed there and many times, because of space, the nonprint materials the students should access are found there also. Ideally, these materials are easily accessible to the students and the professional staff.

The electronic materials should be identified and their locations noted. Are they available on all of the computers in the library? Are they available throughout the school? Are they available from home or other locations outside of school? The inventory list will be helpful in identifying these materials. Although these items are not physical, they need to be identified so that the school librarian understands that they are part of the vast array of resources for the students.

STEP 2: DIVIDE THE COLLECTION INTO SMALLER PARTS

School librarians must determine how to work with the items in the collection. One easy way is to divide the collection through the built-in divisions found in the classification system the school library is using. Many schools are still using the Dewey Decimal systems although alternative configurations of organizing print materials have become popular in some areas. Some schools and public libraries are organizing print materials by a genre-based system (Bucher, 2013).

The task of dividing the collection into manageable parts seems fairly straightforward, but the school librarian does have decisions to make. The following questions need to be answered.

- Will I look at all of the larger sections together?
- Should I tackle all of the 550s (earth sciences and geology) together?
- How about the 900s (History, Travel and Geography)?
- Should I separate the 973s into one area because American history is fairly extensive?
- What should I do about the biographies?
- Should I consider them within a Dewey number or should I use their 92 or 920 designation?
- If this is an elementary school, what should I do with the "easy nonfiction"?
- How about the "easy fiction"?
- What about fiction in general?

All of these questions should be reflected on and considered prior to beginning this project.

Another deciding factor is the school level. If the collection map is being constructed for an elementary school, the items in the Dewey divisions will be different from a middle school or a high school. For example, although American history is studied at all levels, the collections will be more extensive in the middle and high schools. There will be many more materials about dinosaurs in an elementary school than in a high school. Why do such differences need to be considered when thinking about dividing the collection? The purpose of dividing the collection at all is to make it easier to tackle specific sections of the collection without considering all of the items at one time. Determining what to do with 500 items in a section is easier and more time efficient than looking at all 10,000 items in the entire collection. The school librarian should estimate how large each section will be as this initial planning is taking place. Table 5.2 has a possible breakdown for a typical middle school if it is using the Dewey Decimal Classification System. The sections will change using other classification systems.

In addition to determining how the fiction and nonfiction materials will be divided and considered, the school librarian must decide how to look at the electronic and nonprint materials. On the one hand, it is good to consider all of the content of the resources available to the students, but it is also good to know whether the content is contained in a book or in another format. It may be more workable to look at the print items separately and then tackle the electronic resources. School librarians will need to decide which method works best for their school. However, when creating a collection development plan, the data concerning these resources should be combined. Collection Development Plans will be discussed in Chapter 6.

Table 5.2   Possible Dewey Divisions

000s, 100s, 200s	
300s and 400s	Large section of fairy tales
500s	Large section on birds and animals
600s	Large section on inventions and technology Medical ... diseases
700s	Sports
800s	Poetry
900	American history Travel
92 and 920s	If biographies are not filed in the content area number. Mathematicians in the math area, etc.
Fiction	Breakdowns of story collections, any special subject areas ... science fiction, Newbury and Caldecott, graphic novels.
Nonprint materials	
Electronic resources	

STEP 3: DECIDE WHICH PARTS OF THE COLLECTION TO ANALYZE FIRST

Deciding on the initial part to tackle in analyzing a collection may be straightforward. The logical place to begin is with updating the science area or the technology area. Although this is a good course of action, there might be extenuating circumstances that cause the school librarian to select another area first. If the school is embarking on a specific initiative related to student learning, and the library resources play a role in the success of this learning initiative, then this section should be considered first. If the school leadership team has determined that to support the current standards movement, more emphasis should be placed on math resources, the school librarian should then consider updating this area first. Another situation facing the school librarian may be that the school has received funds for updating the Literary Criticism resources. This fact would help guide the school librarian toward that section first. Each one of these items should be considered as the school librarian develops a plan to evaluate the collection.

STEP 4: DETERMINE THE NUMBER OF ITEMS IN A SECTION

If the school library is automated, the easiest way to find the number of items in a section is by creating an inventory report of the specific area being evaluated. It might be a good idea to simply run a full inventory as the school librarian will need the total number of items in each section as the collection mapping process progresses. Some automated programs do not include this inventory function and are rather a circulation module only. The school librarian should contact some of the larger book vendors supplying school library materials and determine if the vendor provides this as a free service. The vendor will need access to the electronic data for the items in the collection or a list of materials in the collection. With this information the vendor should be able to generate a list of the materials broken down by Dewey Decimal or section number. Working with a vendor to compile this information is the easiest and quickest way to gather these data.

A more difficult and time-consuming method is to count the number of items in the section through a printed list or through what is called a catalog shelf list. Another tried-but-true, old-fashioned way is to count the items on the shelves for the designated section or estimate the number of books on the shelf and multiply this by the number of shelves in the section. Regardless of the method used, the resulting data are the number of items in the complete section. The total number or the estimate of the total number of items is important to give the school librarian a better sense of the size of the section in relationship to the other sections in the collection.

STEP 5: PRINT A LIST OF HOLDINGS AND MATCH THE LIST WITH THE ITEMS ON THE SHELF

Armed with the list, the school librarian can now match the items on the list with the items on the shelf. This process, although simple, will provide sufficient data for the school librarian to locate each item in the section and determine if it is on the shelf, missing, or checked out. If the book is missing, this should be noted on the list. If the item is checked out, the school librarian must decide how he or she will snag the item when it is returned to the library. This process may be as simple as informing the people working the circulation desk that the school librarian needs to see every book in that specific section when it is returned to the library. The members of the library staff may use a book cart for harvesting all of these items. The librarian can then retrieve the items that have not gone through the inventory process from the circulation area to finish the evaluation of every book before it is shelved.

STEP 6: EVALUATE EACH ITEM THROUGH QUANTITATIVE MEASURES

Using the information the school librarian has from the total number of items in the section, there are quantitative data that should be gathered. The total number of books per student in the entire collection and then in this section in particular should be determined. Using the list of items in the collection, the school librarian should divide the number of books in the total collection by the number of students in the school. To determine the number of items

Table 5.3   Copyright Tabulation

1970s	1980s	1990s	2000s	2010s
III	IIII	⦀ IIII	⦀ ⦀ II	⦀ ⦀

per student in a specific section, the number of books in the section should be divided by the number of books in the section with the total number of students in the school. For example, if there are 900 students in a middle school and the number of books and other resources in the collection is 15,300, divide 15,300 items by 900 students:

$$15,300 \div 900 = 17.$$

In the total collection, there are 17 books per student. This quantitative information is valuable when developing the collection development plan.

To find the number of books per student in the section, divide the number of items in the section by the number of students. If there are 2,250 books in the section, then there would be 2,250 ÷ 900 = 2.5 books per student in this specific section. Knowing the books per student in a specific section provides good information if the section is a very large one. For example, if the school librarian needed to know the number of fiction books per student in the entire collection, then this answer would be relevant. If the section is very small the number is not as telling. If the section has only 50 books (maybe the 100s or the 000s) then having less than one book per student does not give a realistic picture.

Another quantitative piece of information needed for a collection map is the average copyright date of the items in the section. If the school librarian is using an electronic means of gathering data, this information will be readily available. If, however, this information is not available, then a chart similar to the one in Table 5.3 should be used.

For each item, the school librarian would place a hash mark or tally in the decade that corresponds with the item's copyright date. The previous sample shows that more than half of the items for this section were purchased after the year 2000. In fact, 22 of the 38 items, or 58%, have been purchased since 2000. From this chart, the school librarian has a visual representation of how old or current the collection is.

Knowing the average copyright date of the items in the section the school librarian is evaluating will provide a good picture of the currency of the collection. When discussing the copyright date, several factors should be considered. If the section is one that contains history, then the copyright date is not as important as it would be in evaluating a science collection. The school librarian will need to be aware of the guidelines for materials in the specific portion of the collection being evaluated. Evaluation of the copyright date will be addressed in the next chapter when the process of collection development is analyzed. Right now, it is important to learn the skills of creating the collection map.

A third piece of data important to know about each item is the number of times an item has circulated. This information is available through the circulation records. A circulation report should be run to obtain this information looking at the total circulation statistics and disaggregating the data by each specific section breakdown.

STEP 7: PHYSICAL CONDITION THROUGH QUALITATIVE INFORMATION

Now the school librarian must evaluate each item in the section individually by determining its physical condition. The following questions should be asked and answered if the item being examined is print material:

- Does the book have an interesting appearance?
- Does it have all of its pages?
- Is it free from gum or other foreign substances between the pages?
- Are any of the pages torn?
- Does the book smell or have any unpleasant odors emanating from the pages?
- Are the pages yellow?
- Is the cover undamaged?

If the item is in another physical format, determine if the item is in workable condition and has a pleasant appearance. A good question to ask about any item is: Would I want to check out this item and use it myself or have my children use it? If the answer to this question is, "no," then this item should receive a low rating.

Examining the physical appearance of each of these items provides qualitative data, but the school librarian should have a numerical scale associated with the evaluation of the item. Labeling the item as excellent, good, fair, or poor is subjective. These terms must be defined and have a number associated with each definition. For example, "Excellent" may be defined as being in pristine condition, with no torn pages, no dirt smudges, and no folded corners or pages. "Good" could be defined as a clean item with no torn or folded pages and only a few dirt smudges. Other levels would include designations such as fair or poor so that the school librarian has a rating scale from a pristine book to one that is in extremely poor physical condition. Numbers should then be assigned to each level and an evaluative rating scale is developed. Table 5.4 gives an example of such a scale.

Assigning these numerical ratings to each item provides data the school librarian needs to make judgments as whether to keep the book in the collection, try to replace it, or eliminate it altogether. Using a rating scale provides a numerical value that makes qualitative data more objective. These objective data give a clearer picture of the condition of the resource. If school librarians remain in the same school for a few years, it is conceivable that they will need to remove the items that were purchased since they were hired. Sometimes this is hard because when the resource was purchased, it contained the perfect information that was needed for a specific assignment or content area. Now that resource has a dirty cover and torn pages and must be considered for removal.

Table 5.4   Indicators of Quality

Rating	Description	Numerical Value
Excellent	In pristine condition. No torn or folded pages; no dirt marks; no gum or other foreign substance on item. Item looks like it is a new addition with few circulations.	5
Good	Item is clean with no dirt smudges or marks, no folded or torn pages.	4
Fair	Item has a few tears and smudges. All pages are present and book is readable.	3
Poor	Item is ragged, with torn and folded pages. Has some smudges; no odors or foreign substances present.	2
Unacceptable	This item should not be in the collection. The item has no shelf appeal: torn and folded pages; unpleasant odors; gum and other substances stuck in the pages.	1

It is easier to remove items that one has inherited instead of eliminating the items the school librarian purchased for the collection. No one wants to eliminate a book as books have a sacredness about them. They contain knowledge and we as educators are in the process of making this knowledge available to everyone. How can we be the ones to eliminate any of those items? But the school librarian must remove or replace the resource if it is in poor condition or no longer fits with the curriculum.

STEP 8: EVALUATE THE CONTENT OF THE MATERIAL THROUGH WEEDING

The process of weeding involves more than assessing the physical condition of the book. The content of the resource needs to be evaluated. Each book should be examined to determine if the information is outdated, contains inaccurate information, does not support the collection, or has been superseded by a revised or updated version (Bishop, 2013). Through weeding the school librarian determines the accuracy and relevancy of the information for the members of the learning community. A judgment is then made on each item determining if it still "fits" into the collection.

The content of each resource should be up-to-date and relevant. It should be free from bias and stereotypes. It should be accurate. To evaluate the items in the collection, the school librarian must know the content of the books and the accuracy of the information, must understand the curriculum and what is covered through the curriculum, and must understand the reading levels of the students and of the materials. All of this information is needed to decide if the item should remain in the collection or not. This content analysis takes more time than a physical review of the item itself.

Many resources are available that will assist the school librarian with this process (Bishop 2013; Evans & Saponaro, 2005; Johnson, 2009). In fact, any collection development resource will address the concept of weeding. Many librarians use the CREW method, CREW standing for: Continuous Review Evaluation and Weeding. This method was originally published in 1995 and has recently been revised and expanded to include e-books (Larson, 2012). This manual provides step-by-step guidelines to evaluate materials by physical appearance, which we have already addressed, content, subject area, and copyright date. CREW uses a formula that includes the age of the book, the length of time since the item has circulated, and various negative factors identified through the acronym, MUSTIE, which stands for Misleading, Ugly, Superseded, Trivial, Irrelevant, Elsewhere. The CREW manual provides examples of how the MUSTIE can be employed. In addition, the CREW manual provides formulas addressing these issues for each of the Dewey Decimal classes. The CREW manual also has sections on various nonprint sources, e-books, fiction, nonfiction, and children's and adult materials. A copy of the CREW Manual is available on the Texas State Library and Archives Commission Website: https://www.tsl.texas.gov/ld/pubs/crew/index.html.

Using the age of the book, the circulation record, and MUSTIE, a CREW formula could look like this: 7/4/MUT = the item is seven years old, it hasn't circulated in four years, the content is misleading, the volume is ugly, and the content is trivial, important in the 1950s but not in the 2000s.

Another value of the CREW Manual is that each Dewey class has a guideline attached. The Dewey 520s (Space and Astronomy) have 5/3/MUSTIE, but the 510s (Mathematics) have 10/3/MUSTIE. When weeding the Space and Astronomy materials, if the item is five years old and has not circulated in the last three years, and has any of the MUSTIE criteria present, it is a candidate for removal from the collection. However, the mathematics books with a copyright date that is 10 years old could still be relevant, depending on the MUSTIE factors. School librarians should remember, though, that these are guidelines only. School librarians must determine if the CREW guidelines fit with the collection development policy they have for their school. The CREW method is a well-respected way of evaluating items in the collection. School librarians should review the manual and determine its value to their collection.

As school librarians begin weeding a specific area of the collection, they must develop guidelines for their individual library programs. School librarians should develop a weeding policy that states explicitly how this process will be followed in the school library. Items that should be addressed in this policy are: the process of weeding; the schedule of weeding; the person responsible for weeding the collection; the person responsible for making the decisions for weeded items; how to dispose the items; how the items will be replaced.

WHAT DOES ALL OF THIS MEAN?

In this chapter we have discussed the process of collection mapping. Collection mapping is a means of figuring out what resources are in a collection and how relevant they are for the instructional program in the school. Collection mapping includes a way of evaluating the collection both quantitatively and qualitatively to ascertain what resources are available and which resources should be removed from the collection. School librarians need to plan how they will develop a collection map (Steps 1-8), remove the weeded materials (Step 9), and reflect this information on the actual map (Step 10). The school librarians should compare the results of the collection map with the information they gathered from the teachers through their curriculum maps. With all of this information, school librarians will continue establishing their leadership roles as information specialists and become more astute curriculum partners with the teachers in their school. To effectively complete the collecting mapping process, school librarians will need to juggle many tasks, but the resulting benefit will outweigh the steps in the journey.

Reflective Questions

Thinking of your own school library, which section of the resources would you evaluate first and why?

How would you apply the weeding process to nonprint and digital materials?

What classification system would you like to use in your library and why?

Why is a collection map important?

How would you explain the importance of the collection map to your principal?

How would you explain the importance of a collection map to the teachers?

Explain the relationship between a curriculum map and a collection map?

How can school librarians exhibit their leadership skills in working with the administrators and faculty on developing a collection map?

Chapter 6

Collection Development

After studying this chapter, the school librarian will understand the concept of collection development, be able to articulate a method of developing a collection, and understand the necessity of having a living collection development plan.

Curriculum mapping, collection mapping, and collection development are closely related and create the means of evaluating, selecting, and budgeting materials for the school library collection. Curriculum mapping and collection mapping occur in cycles and to implement both items require thinking, reflecting, and planning in a logical manner. In the last few chapters, we looked at how the school librarian works with teachers to assist and complete both a curriculum map and a collection map. The information gathered through both of these processes presents an overview of the curriculum for each grade level and a means of evaluating the items in a school library collection. But the cycle is not yet complete. Now the school librarian must use these data to create a collection development policy. This policy will ensure the collection will evolve in a logical and vibrant manner.

WHAT IS COLLECTION DEVELOPMENT?

When a student walks into the library and asks for materials on a subject, the school librarian wants to provide the resources the student needs. The mechanism for providing the requested materials for the student begins with collection development. Collection development is the process of being prepared so that the right materials are available for students to access when that information is needed. But this condition doesn't occur without a significant amount of prior planning. To create a collection that provides learners with the information they need, different events need to occur. Various authors have addressed the process of collection development from different points of view, which describe different methods and procedures and provide tips to assist with this process (Bishop, 2013; Doll & Barron, 2002; Evans & Saponaro,

55

Table 6.1   Steps in Creating a Collection Development Plan

Steps in Creating a Collection Development Plan
1. Learning the Collection
2. Conducting a needs assessment
3. Selecting the Materials
4. Creating the Plan

2005; Mardis, 2015; Morris, 2010; Woolls, Weeks, & Coatney, 2014). Although the flavor of each of these authors is different, the basic intent is to develop a plan that will establish the procedures to create a collection that supports the needs of the students and the curriculum design of the school. There are certain steps that the school librarian should follow in developing this plan, which include: learning the collection; conducting a needs assessment; and locating and selecting the materials. (See Table 6.1.)

LEARNING THE COLLECTION

In Chapter 5, Collection Mapping, the process of evaluating the collection by means of collection mapping was described. The school librarian may not always have the time or opportunity to follow the steps in evaluating the collection prior to developing a collection development plan. If that is the case, then the school librarian must use other tactics to learn as much about the collection as possible in the shortest amount of time.

What materials are currently in the school library collection? Answering this should be one of the first steps a librarian takes when learning about the collection or arriving at a school to begin a new position. Different methods can be used to accomplish this task. The school librarian may review the inventory list on the Integrated Library System (ILS) or look at the materials that have circulated. Perusing the cart of returned books to be shelved is another way to familiarize oneself with the collection. The school librarian may want to browse the shelves in different subject areas to see what materials are there. It won't take long to have a general idea of what the collection contains even though the formal evaluation of each item has not occurred.

As the school librarian works with the teachers and attends their planning sessions, it will become clear where materials are lacking. Students will certainly provide the school librarian with information about what is missing in the collection. A vital aspect of getting familiar with the collection is to find out what is physically in the collection, what is virtually available, and also to discuss with the students and the teachers what should be there. The school librarian should check any previously developed curriculum maps and compare them with the materials in the collection. This comparison will help the school librarian when initiating the process of collection mapping, which will paint a clear picture of robust subject areas and areas where resources are lacking.

This process is workable for the physical materials in the collection, but the school librarian must also learn what electronic materials are available. If the school has any type of electronic resources, the school librarian should note the titles and determine if there are duplicates in the print collection. The databases should be reviewed as well as any other electronic sources, such as encyclopedias that are part of the collection, so that a determination can be made if there are any yearly electronic subscriptions that are part of the library resources.

With the explosion of electronic sources, information professionals are organizing electronic content into specific subject areas, gathering the most relevant sources, and saving them as a digital artifact in one of the many social media sites. Bhargava (2011) defines the organizing of electronic items on one topic as content curation. By curating these items, school librarians create a digital file with relevant material on one subject. When school librarians are learning the collection, they must also review these curated materials to ascertain how they fit into the overall collection.

CONDUCTING A NEEDS ASSESSMENT

Evaluating all of these types of resources gives a good picture of the breadth of the collection, but it may not dig down and see the depth of the materials available. The challenge the school librarian faces is determining whether or not the resources in the collection are really what the students need either for their classes or for their own information needs. In addition to the students, the needs of the faculty and the members of the learning community should be considered. To determine how the collection aligns with the needs of all of these users, the school librarian must conduct a needs analysis or needs assessment. This process might also be called a community analysis, a user analysis, or an environmental scan. Regardless of the term or the shades of difference in the meanings, data painting a picture of the users, the school, the community, and their information needs must be collected.

Data Areas

Detailed information about the learning community should be collected. Major data collection divisions include school characteristics, district configurations, and community information. Looking at the needs of the learning community through the school lens necessitates collecting data on students, teachers, the plan of study, and school configuration. Student enrollment, the ratio of students to teaching staff, and administrators should be noted. The students' personal and academic interests, examining the electives in the curriculum, the extracurricular activities students support and attend, and the popularity of many of the after school clubs and events illustrate some of the interests students share. Looking at the teachers and staff members through the same lens will show what the faculty support and where their interests lie. Data should also be collected concerning the structure of the classes in the school, the configuration of the classrooms, and the demographics of the student body.

What is the school district like? How large is it? How many schools? What is the configuration of the schools? What is the governance of the schools? Is the district collaborative or does it have top-down management? The answers to all of these questions will illustrate how the school district works and will give the school librarian a better idea of the culture in the school district and how that aligns with the school program.

Data on the district and the school are fairly easy to obtain from reports on the district and school websites and through the Department of Education in each state. The National Center for Education Statistics (NCES) (Institute of Education Sciences, 2015) provides statistical data related to education. The database is searchable by school, public or private, by district, and by colleges and universities. NCES provides complete data that one can use for a needs assessment of a specific school and will also provide information about the school district. Additional means of collecting this data for the school is through an electronic school report card available on the district website or through an Internet search. All of these data will paint a complete picture of the school and the district.

Another lens used to collect data is through a picture of the community. What type of community is this: rural, urban, suburban? What is the economic status of the members of the community? What resources are available for the students and the parents who live in the community? Are there public libraries and special libraries where the members of the learning community have access to specific resources? This information can be obtained from the city or county website, the local Chamber of Commerce, local state agencies or government agencies in the area. A list of the local clubs and recreational facilities can be found on the websites or often are advertised in the public libraries in the area.

In addition to collecting these data through websites, electronic resources, and printed information, simple surveys can be created to give to both students and community members. The student surveys should be designed to determine the students' area of interest. They could also help determine the educational areas the students wish to explore further. School librarians should also gather this information through more informal means such as talking with the students to see their interests. Bishop (2013) includes sample questions that are appropriate for gathering this information and also encourages the use of questions that are easily understood by the students so the data collected will guide the school librarian.

With all of these data, the school librarian will have a good idea of the school, the district, the community, and the members that makeup the community. This information will paint a picture for the school librarian of the resources available and will describe the needs of the members of the learning community. Table 6.2 enumerates other possible sources of data to gather to create this mosaic of the learning community. School librarians must use every possible source of information to identify and synthesize the needs of the community and the resources available.

Table 6.2 Data Collection Sources

School Characteristics—Students	School Characteristics—Teachers and Curriculum
Approximate enrollment Student interests, both school and personal Grouping of students (grade level, subject matter, tracking, multiage, or similar configurations) Special Populations (physically challenged, learning disabled, gifted, bilingual) Extracurricular activities for students	Number of teachers and administrators Types and number of special teachers (music, art, reading ESL, bilingual, technology) Subjects taught or emphasized in the curriculum Standards used in the school (state, common core) Special subjects teachers emphasize Outside interest of teachers Educational background of teachers and administrators Teaching techniques used (teaming, small group, cooperative learning, professional learning communities; communities of practice) Special learning approaches (STEM, STEAM, reading across the curriculum, balanced literacy, common core, whole language)
District Characteristics	**Community Characteristics**
Size and number of other schools in the district Geographical areas (rural, urban, suburban) School library support personnel and resources Resource sharing between schools Collaboration between schools Management characteristics (site based, collaborative decision making, central control)	Population (current distribution and possible shifts that may occur) Age distribution Racial/ethnic composition Economic background (tax base, economic levels, employment levels) Occupations Religious affiliations—predominantly one sect or another Family structure (one parent, two parents, blended families)
Community Resources	
Public Libraries Bookmobile services University and special libraries Government and public service resources Community centers and recreational facilities	

SELECTING THE MATERIALS

The third integral step of collection development determines how to select the materials to make the collection more robust and reflective of the needs of the members of the learning community. These data will show the gaps in the materials, and the school librarian must then decide what types of materials should be selected to shore up the areas of weakness. As these decisions are made, they should be reflected in a policy that will guide the acquisition of materials.

This document will become the collection development policy. Having a method for selecting materials is part of that plan. Some libraries have a specific selection policy that governs the process of developing the collection. The selection process or policy is under the umbrella of collection development and, whether it is labeled as a policy or a process, selection must be considered in the entire collection development list of activities.

The question is: How do school librarians select materials for the school library? Where do they start? What process should be followed? What tools are available to assist the school librarian in selecting materials? All of these are great questions and the answers need to be determined and analyzed as the school librarian begins selecting materials.

Selecting materials for a school library encompasses more than the school library itself. We have already seen that the school librarian must identify users' needs and wants, and we have discussed ways of gathering this information. The school district must be involved in this process also. The first step in determining how to select materials and what materials to select is looking at the policies of the school district and reviewing any existing policies that have been approved by the school board. An in-depth review of the board policies is a good place to start. If this search of existing policy is not fruitful, the school librarian can work with the district school library supervisor, curriculum director, district legal team, or secretary of the school board to determine if a thorough search has been completed. If a policy is already in existence, then the school librarian should use this policy as a template for the school's process of selection. If there is no policy, the school librarian should work with his or her administrator and faculty to develop a policy that is appropriate for their school. This school level policy could become the nucleus for a district policy.

These items should be considered when looking at selecting materials for the school library. The data that were collected will give a direction for the content; however, in selecting the actual items, the AASL (2009) guidelines from *Empowering Learner: Guidelines for School Librarians* should be considered: the materials in the collection should include different formats, support for the curriculum, and the information needs of the students. In reflecting on this statement, notice must be given to a variety of formats that address a wide range of subject areas appropriate for different learning styles, diverse backgrounds, and specific age levels. Selection procedures also include looking at the quality of the item, its durability, the price, its appeal to the user, its relevance to the curriculum, its reading level, and a host of additional factors

(Gregory, 2011; Morris, 2010; Woolls, et al., 2014). In essence, the selection policy or procedure should address the philosophy of selecting materials, identifying who is responsible for the selection of materials, and the criteria for each type of format selected (Howard, 2011).

SO, WHAT SHOULD I PURCHASE?

The answer to this is in the data, at least for the content. In Chapter 5, Collection Mapping, we outlined the process of "weeding" and, by using this practice, school librarians gain a better idea of what resources were eliminated and where the content gaps are. They should also compare parts of the collection with the curriculum maps they have received from the teachers. The formats that are already in the library collection should be evaluated to see if they need to be updated to more relevant technology or if budget funds should be allotted to purchase additional items. To summarize, school librarians need to look at:

- The gaps in the curriculum
- The content of the weeded materials
- The relevance of the existing formats
- The possibility of any new curriculum being implemented
- The needs of the students and the faculty

In addition, other decisions also need to be made.

- What type of binding does the library want to purchase for the book resources?
- Should the library purchase the same type of electronic formats or should funds be allotted for other formats?
- Should funds be allocated for the existing databases and electronic resources or would new subscriptions be more appropriate?
- Should duplicate copies of books be purchased?
- Should multiple licenses be purchased for various pieces of software, electronic books, or access to databases?

Although the list of questions seems endless, the bottom line is that the library budget limits the funds available to the school librarian to update, replace, add to, and expand the library resources. A priority list needs to be developed to stretch the power of the funds in the budget.

GIFTS

Another situation that often arises is that of donated materials and gifts from members of the learning community. School librarians need to have a clear policy as to how these items will be handled. A few years ago, I was cleaning out my personal library and decided that the textbooks I used when working on my master's degree were no longer relevant, and I could remove them from my collection. My first thought was to donate them to the local public library. However, it didn't take me long to realize that the public library would not want these outdated tomes, and I should eliminate them in some other manner. This same scenario often takes place when members of the learning community want to donate various materials to the school library. Their intentions are commendable, but the materials may not fit into the school library collection. Therefore, having a policy of established criteria about gifts and donations allows the school librarians to make appropriate decisions and still show appreciation for the donor's thoughtfulness. The school librarian should consider the following:

- Does the material support the curriculum of the school?
- Does the material support the school's selection policy?

By answering these two questions, the school librarian can determine whether the items should be accepted as part of the collection. If the materials do not support these criteria, then the school librarian should thank the donor and say that although the materials may not fit in this school library's collections they will be shared with other libraries. It is important to acknowledge the generosity of the members of the learning community but realize all gifts do not or should not be accepted if they do not support the selection policy.

BABY STEPS, AGAIN

The concept of baby steps was discussed in the context of changing the school culture in Chapter 3. It is worth mentioning again as baby steps should be the philosophy of all school librarians when they try to develop the best collection possible. The amount of the budgetary money is not going to stretch as far as the needs so the school librarian must have a solid list of priorities. As decisions are made about what to purchase and in what format, the amount of budget should be fresh in the school librarian's mind. Various authors (Bishop, 2013; Gregory, 2011; Kimmel, 2014) have identified the advantages and disadvantages of different formats and resources. The school librarian should make decisions about the collection using these published guidelines.

POLICIES AND PROCEDURES

The school librarian now knows the collection, has conducted a needs assessment, and has determined what materials should be selected. The next step is to develop a plan that will provide the means to implement existing policies and procedures developed for the school library. Before analyzing the parts of this collection development plan, the school librarian must have a clear idea of what a policy is and what procedures are. A policy is a rule that guides the direction of an organization. It reflects the mission and goals of the organization and gives the leaders a blueprint to carry out their established functions. In a school district, the school board has the responsibility for establishing its governing policies. These policies form the backbone of the rules and regulations of the school district. To implement these governance policies, procedures need to be established. Procedures provide the means to implement the policies. Policies are established, approved, and implemented. To change a policy, the school board needs to discuss the ramifications of the changes, decide on whether they believe these changes will support the mission and goals of the district, and then vote on whether to accept and implement the changes. Procedures, on the other hand, may be changed if there is reason to believe a better, more efficient way to enact a policy can be established.

Individual schools may also create policies that will govern their specific mission and goals, and the school may develop procedures to implement these policies. Following this format, individual departments in the school may also develop and implement policies and the procedures to carry out those policies. The school library has an advisory board that will assist in the policy development and implementation of established procedures. The school librarian needs to work with the library advisory committee to develop a policy and procedures manual, and it is in this manual that the collection development policy is often found.

COLLECTION DEVELOPMENT PLAN CONTENT

Policies

The collection development plan includes both policies and procedures. The policies address any appropriate school board policies that govern the acquisition and selection for materials to be used in the schools; the deselection of materials; and any ancillary policy that will address resources or access to those resources. This plan must also include national policies that address selection, access, and use of resources in the school district both in the classroom and the school library. The school librarians should search their School Board policies and compare these policies to national organizations such as the American Library Association (ALA). If ALA has policies regarding access and selection of materials and these policies are missing at the school district level, the school librarian must explore the process of having these seminal policies approved by the school board. Both the school board policies and the appropriate ALA policies should be referred to in the collection development plan. Some possible policies to include in the collection development plan are listed in Table 6.3.

Table 6.3 Sample Governing Policies

National Organizations	Possible School Board Policies
American Library Association Library Bill of Rights • Include resources regardless of the origin or background of the author • Include resources that present various points of view • Avoid censorship of materials, including self-censorship • Provide free access to materials • Support the tenets of intellectual freedom **National Council for the Teachers of English** • Intellectual Freedom Policy • Reconsideration of Materials Policy	**Instructional Materials** Selection Approval **Challenge to Instructional Materials and Activities** Policy Procedure for challenging materials

Procedures

Collection development plans should address any issue or explain any facet of how a collection is developed that pertains to the school and the learning community. Bishop (2013, pp. 37–43) provides detailed information about how to write a collection development plan along with a policies and procedurals manual. The major items to be addressed in a plan are: the mission of the school library, the members of the learning community, the procedures for selecting and deselecting materials, the types of materials, the issues of gifts, and how to address challenges to the materials. The school librarians should think about how detailed they want the procedures that accompany the policies in the manual. These decisions must be considered because school librarians need a roadmap when they are developing the collection. The Policy and Procedures Manual will provide transparency for the administrators, teachers, staff, and members of the learning community as to how the school librarian is providing the resources to satisfy students' information needs.

Table 6.4 provides guiding questions the school librarians should ponder as they begin preparing the Policies and Procedures Manual. School librarians should reflect on the answers to each of these questions because they will often provide the blueprint for a robust collection development plan.

WHAT DOES ALL OF THIS MEAN?

The last few chapters have identified three different concepts: curriculum mapping, collection mapping, and collection development. School librarians are involved in all three processes and at each juncture exhibit their leadership roles. In curriculum mapping, they work closely with teachers to understand the curriculum framework and its implementation at each grade level and in each classroom. In collection mapping, the school librarians determine the

Table 6.4   Guiding Questions

Mission Statement	Members of the Learning Community
What is the mission statement of the library?	From the results of the needs assessment, what should be the focus of the materials for the school library? Is there any specific grade level or curriculum content that should be addressed?
Selection of materials What types of formats should be selected? How much of the budget will be for books? How much of the budget will be used for electronic resources? What selection tools should be used? Who has the final say in the items that will be purchased?	**Deselection of materials** Is there a type of format that should be eliminated from the collection because of being outdated? What process should be used to deselect materials? How should deselected materials be disposed?
Types of materials What types of materials will be purchased for the school library collection? What type of bindings should be purchased? How many copies of each book should be purchased? What criteria should be used for purchasing electronic materials or electronic subscriptions?	**Gifts** Should gifts be accepted for the school library collection? If the library decides to accept gifts, what procedures should be established concerning these items? If items are given to the school library that do not fit the content of the school library, how should these items be disposed?
Reconsiderations of materials What is the process for reconsidering materials for the library? What is the process for reconsidering materials for the classroom? What steps should be followed to address a challenge to the materials available through the library? What steps should be followed to address a challenge to the materials available through the classroom?	

resources that are available in their individual schools. Collection development includes learning the collection, understanding the diversity of the community, and determining the selection criteria for additional resources. Collection development includes establishing an overall written plan that includes policies and procedures that will guide the school librarian in developing a vibrant collection. At each step in curriculum mapping, collection mapping, and collection development, school librarians assume leadership roles to guarantee that the plans are developed and implemented. All three items involve working with administrators, faculty, and members of the community to retrieve the needed information. As instructional leaders, school librarians will accomplish these tasks.

Reflective Questions

What is the relationship among curriculum mapping, collection mapping, and collection development?

What leadership skills will you need to employ to accomplish curriculum mapping, collection mapping, and collection development?

What policies need to be included in a collection development plan?

What decisions will you make about selecting materials in for your school library?

How will you present the collection development policy to your principal?

How will you present the collection development policy to your faculty?

What steps will you take to conduct a needs assessment in your community?

7

Instructional Partner and Change

After studying this chapter, the reader will understand the role of the school librarian as an instructional partner and how that role has evolved through the years. The role will be analyzed through the lens of the process of change.

In Chapter 4, Curriculum Mapping, we met two middle school teachers from different subject areas: one from social studies and one from language arts, who contacted the school librarian to work on separate current issue assignments. The culminating project for each assignment was an oral speech. However, the two teachers were isolated in their own classrooms and concentrated, exclusively, on their individual curriculum content. This isolationism contributed to the school librarian being unsuccessful in convincing the two teachers to work together. This event occurred in the 1990s before school librarians embraced the role of instructional partner. The school librarian would have approached the situation differently if it had occurred after the implementation of *Empowering Learners, Guidelines for School Library Programs* (AASL, 2009). Instead of suggesting the teachers work together, the school librarian would create a three-person collaborative relationship: The social studies teacher, the language arts teacher, and the school librarian. This collaborative unit would allow the school librarian to be an instructional partner with the two classroom teachers.

A BRIEF HISTORY OF THE INSTRUCTIONAL ROLE

The instructional role of the school librarian is present in the earliest standards. The standards in the 1920s and 1930s state that school librarians should be an integral part of the school and that their responsibilities include teaching students and supplementing their instruction (Roscello, 2004). In the 1950s, schools placed more emphasis on learning and methods of delivering instruction, and this change allowed the school librarian more opportunities to be involved with curriculum development (Carver, 1986). Roscello and

Carver both provide detailed information about the various iterations of standards and guidelines affecting the school library profession. A close reading of these standards and guidelines will trace the evolution of the school librarian's different roles. We will review the three most recent standards and guidelines to paint a picture of the current roles and responsibilities in the curriculum area.

INFORMATION POWER: GUIDELINES FOR SCHOOL LIBRARY MEDIA PROGRAMS (1988)

In 1988 the American Association of School Librarians (AASL) and the Association of Educational Communications and Technology (AECT) published *Information Power: Guidelines for School Library Media Programs*. This document evolved from the previous standards published in 1960, 1969, and 1975 and continued the evolution of the school librarian's instructional role [American Association of School Librarians (AASL) & Association of Educational Communications and Technology (AECT), 1988]. The purpose of this document was to illustrate how school librarians could provide additional access to and use of information to the members of the learning community. *Information Power* describes the roles of the school librarian as information specialist, teacher, and instructional consultant (p. 26). The instructional consultant role addresses the school librarian's responsibility of serving on curriculum committees at the school and the district levels, suggesting sources that could be used in the classroom introducing information literacy skills into the curriculum, and presenting instruction to assist teachers in learning about the existing emerging technologies. The school librarian should work with teachers individually to provide recommendations as to curriculum content and assist with the instructional design of the lessons. School librarians should also develop school-wide programs involving all grade levels. This instructional consultant role described the school librarian as one who provided support but was still on the periphery of the instructional program.

INFORMATION POWER: BUILDING PARTNERSHIPS FOR LEARNING (1998)

AASL and AECT revised the 1988 standards and published *Information Power: Building Partnerships for Learning* (AASL & AECT, 1998) and in the process changed the focus of the guidelines. The 1998 guidelines emphasized student learning and the responsibility that school librarians have in preparing students to become lifelong learners. During the ten years between these two publications, *Information Power* (1988) and *Information Power* (1998), the infusion of technology permeated society, and the means of accessing information increased exponentially. Preparing students to become lifelong learners through understanding, knowing, and accepting the information literacy standards became the goal of school librarians everywhere. School librarians had the responsibility of working with teachers to make certain that students gained the information literacy skills they needed by accessing this information through a variety of resources. In the second *Information Power* (1998), the school librarian's roles were identified as Teacher, Instructional Partner, Information Specialist, and Program Administrator. It should be noted that the Instructional Consultant role in the 1988 standards was changed to Instructional Partner in 1998. This change in name reflects the thinking that school librarians need to be more than "consultants" finding information and resources for teachers, to "partners" working hand in hand with the teachers to integrate the information literacy standards into the classroom curriculum. This change of title may seem insignificant, but in reality it shows that the school librarian needs to work very closely with teachers and members of the learning community to assist students in becoming lifelong learners. School librarians are no longer on the periphery of learning as a consultant would be, but are more involved with the planning and delivery of instruction as a "partner." As instructional partners with teachers, school librarians infuse the information literacy standards into the classroom curriculum. Information literacy is the vehicle necessary in understanding the curriculum content, developing critical thinking skills, and learning how to solve problems (AASL & AECT, 1998). The instructional partner role catapulted the concept of collaboration with classroom teachers to the forefront of the school library program. To be partners, school librarians, need to collaborate closely with teachers in classroom instruction, in the use of appropriate technology, and through the development of authentic lessons. The instructional partner has a closer and more intimate role with the classroom teacher.

EMPOWERING LEARNERS: GUIDELINES FOR SCHOOL LIBRARY PROGRAMS (2009)

In 2006, AASL (2009) convened a Vision Summit that included one school library representative from each of the 50 states. This Summit was the first step in the process of developing new standards and guidelines for school library programs. These guidelines, found in *Empowering Learners: Guidelines for School Library Programs*, reflect the same roles as *Information Power* (1988, 1998) but adds a fifth role of leader (AASL, 2009). In addition, the focus of the school librarian's roles shifted. As *Empowering Learners* was developed, school librarians were asked to rank their common roles. Prior to 2009, the role of teacher was ranked first. With *Empowering Learners*, Instructional Partner is now ranked as number one. This revised ranking does not imply that teaching is not important, it simply illustrates that the role of the school librarian has changed (see Table 7.1).

WHAT DOES INSTRUCTIONAL PARTNER MEAN?

Partners are people who work together with common goals, a shared vision, and equal authority for making the relationship viable. This partnership is often described as being a collaborative relationship, and collaboration has been parsed and analyzed in many ways. A simple definition of collaboration

Table 7.1 Changes in School Librarians' Roles

1988 Information Power	1998 Information Power	2009 Empowering Learners
Stated roles but not in ranked order (p. 26)	Stated roles (pp. 4–5)	Stated roles in ranked order (p. 16)
Information Specialist Teacher Instructional Consultant	Teacher Instructional Partner Information Specialist Program Administrator	Instructional Partner Information Specialist Teacher Program Administrator Additional Role added: Leader

would be more than one person working together to accomplish a goal. This group would need to have a shared vision, common goals and objectives, and the ability to work with trust and respect for each other (Bennis, 2009; Bennis & Nanus, 2003; Collins, 2001; Deal & Peterson, 2009; Grover, 1996; Kouzes & Posner, 2002; Senge, 1990). This concept of collaboration is the bedrock of the instructional partner role.

The concept of school librarians and teachers joining in collaborative relationships is not new. The 1988 DeWitt Wallace-Reader's Digest *Library Power* project (Zweizig & Hopkins, 1999) required the school librarian to work closely with the classroom teacher, collaborating on lessons to infuse information literacy into the content areas. *Power Libraries* (Bankhead, 2003), one program in Colorado that grew out of the *Library Power* project, required that teams consisting of a school librarian, a classroom teacher, and a principal receive training on how to work together as a collaborative team, thus implementing the Instructional Partnership role. The Meeting in the Middle Event in 1995 (Grover, 1996) supported this same configuration of having teams of principals, school librarians, and classroom teachers work together to learn how to prepare collaborative lessons.

In the school library field, collaboration has been defined in different ways. *Information Power, Building Partnerships for Learning* (AASL & AECT, 1998) defines this collaborative role as the school librarian working with teachers to establish this partnership relationship. Grover (1996) identifies collaboration as the integration of information literacy instruction into the classroom curriculum. Montiel-Overall (2005) defines collaboration in the educational area as the process of teachers and school librarians working together to increase student learning.

Implementing a collaborative working relationship is a slow process and can be accomplished in stages: cooperation, coordination, and finally collaboration. Cooperation is the process of working separately but then coming together for the lesson. Each person, the teacher and the school librarian, has his or her own parts and come together only for the actual lesson. Coordination is a more formal approach, and the teacher informs the school librarian as to the parameters of the lesson. The school librarian then decides what information is needed for the students to be successful in their assignment. The difference

Table 7.2 Cooperation, Coordination, and Collaboration

Cooperation	Coordination	Collaboration
A school librarian prepares a lesson on searching for resources through the catalog or electronic databases. The teacher prepares a lesson on the seven continents. The teacher presents the content and then the students go to the library to have the school librarian explain how to use the resources. The students then check out or access appropriate resources to support the concepts of the classroom lesson.	A teacher approaches the school librarian to work with his classes on a research paper. The teacher and the school librarian discuss the focus of the research and the school librarian determines what resources should be presented to the students on their first research day in the library.	The teacher and the school librarian discuss a concept that is curriculum based and determine the goals and objectives for the lesson. They work side by side from the development of the lesson through the final assessment of the students. Together they determine the content, the guiding questions, the end product and the method of assessment.

between these two scenarios is sometimes hard to distinguish. In the coordination stage the two entities need not communicate often or at all, as each knows their material. During the cooperation stage, the school librarian and the teacher need to determine what the content is so that the school librarian can present the appropriate resources. Collaboration is the goal and is achieved when the teacher and school librarian look at a curriculum area, discuss the goals associated with the curriculum, plan the design of the lessons, team-teach, and then assess the students. This event is a complete lesson with two teachers (classroom and school librarian) working as partners to assist the students with authentic learning. Collaboration summarizes the role of the school librarian as an instructional partner. Collaboration is the river, and coordination and cooperation are two tributaries supporting the river. Table 7.2 gives examples of the differences in Cooperation, Coordination, and Collaboration.

A major ingredient of being an instructional partner with teachers is establishing a culture of collaboration. The school librarian becomes so integral to the teaching and learning in the school that processes are established to ensure that this collaborative culture is healthy. One ingredient for establishing this collaborative culture is configuring the school schedule so that the librarian has a flexible schedule and the opportunity to participate in the teachers' common planning periods. If this cannot be accomplished with common planning periods, then creative alternatives should be considered. To be partners, the teachers and the school librarian must have the opportunity to work together for planning purposes, lesson design, and the implementation of the lesson. For a variety of reasons, this planning opportunity does not always occur.

For example, a school librarian recently hired at an elementary school and steeped with the passion and drive to implement the best school library program possible finds after the first few months that teachers are not flocking to the door to suggest the school librarian become partners with them and develop collaborative lessons. This scenario takes place in many schools to varying degrees. The question is: What can a school librarian do to establish his or her role as an instructional partner?

Although the role of the school librarian as an instructional partner is not new, this concept is new to many educators who compare school librarians to the image to those they have worked with in the past. Librarians have been seen as "keepers of the book" and this categorization is often applied to school librarians. However, it is important to take steps to change this image in the learning community.

Many authors have written about the change process and it is linked to the qualities of leadership. The mantra of implementing change is "baby steps" and celebrating successes. Implementing change involves changing the culture of the organization and as discussed in Chapter 3, School Culture and School Relationships, this change process is difficult. However, there are steps that can be followed to help in this process.

CHANGE

Change occurs when a leader or group of leaders convince others that a different course of action should be undertaken. This change may take place by hiring a new principal who changes the focus and direction of the school. Maybe the former principal was a visionary and relished in sharing this vision with the faculty. The new principal emphasizes balancing the budget and the budget is the focus of many discussions with the faculty. This change could be immediate, and the faculty will need to modify their ways of operating. Often the change is not as drastic as hiring a new administrator and may involve only smaller changes in the daily routine. Maybe the bell schedule is changed; teachers have their teaching assignments changed; new teams are formed in the school. Change is inevitable and realizing this is part of the leadership role of the school librarian.

SCHOOL LIBRARIANS IMPLEMENTING CHANGE

To begin the change process, school librarians should gather data and assess the existing school culture (see Chapter 3, School Culture and School Relationships). They should learn the curriculum content, understand the teaching methods of each of the teachers in the school, and determine where possible collaborative partnerships could be developed. School librarians should understand that there are different types of personalities that make up any organization, and this is true of each school unit. Some people are ready for change and embrace it simply because it is change. Others fear change and do not want anything to affect their teaching position or method of working with students.

Many authors have analyzed the different types of people that comprise organizations, and each author analyzes the structure of organizations differently using various metaphors or mental models to assist in understanding how organizations function and address change (Bolman & Deal, 2008; Burns, 1978; Deal and Peterson, 2009; DuFour & Eaker, 1998; Schein, 2010, 1992). Rogers (2003) presents a clear explanation of individuals and how they accept change. Through his diffusion theory he categorizes how people accept an innovation or a change. His description of how individuals adopt change fall into five categories: Innovators, Early Adopters, Early Majority, Late Majority, and Laggards. Innovators think creatively and frequently take risks to implement something new. Early Adopters spend more time analyzing a situation before accepting it as a course of action. Members of the Early Majority group accept an idea before the critical mass of individuals accept it. The Late Majority remains skeptical until the change is implemented, and they can determine if it will be successful or not. The Laggards are the last group, and these individuals make their decisions based on what has been done in the past. If these categories were placed on a continuum, the people who stand in line to be the first to purchase the most innovative piece of technology (Innovators) would be on one end and people who do not yet have a smartphone (Laggards) would be on the other.

As school librarians consider their teachers and administrators, they should be mindful of Rogers's adopter categories to determine if their colleagues belong to one or more of these categories. In determining how to implement the partnership concept with teachers, school librarians should identify the Innovators or Early Majority groups because they are more likely to consider implementing this change. Working with members of these two groups will pave the way for a successful partnership.

Michael Fullan is a change guru in the education field. His works address the process of change for administrators, teachers, and anyone working as a leader in this field. In *Change Forces* (1993) he identifies eight basic lessons about the change process. Two of them are very appropriate for the school librarian to remember. Change cannot be mandated and change is fluid instead of being set in stone. School librarians know what their role is in being a partner with classroom teachers, but they cannot mandate that the teachers accept this role change. This change must be implemented because the teacher understands that this instructional partner role is a good thing; a win/win for the teacher, the school librarian, and, most importantly, for the students. The second basic lesson illustrates that implementing change is a fluid process, one that changes as the school librarian and the teachers interact. The best plan needs to be thought of as a journey to a goal, one of equal partnership, but the process is one that changes with each interaction.

Fullan (2008) also identifies six secrets of success in the change process. Although written mainly for organizational management and school administrators, the school librarian can adapt three of these secrets to the change process for becoming an Instructional Partner. Fullan's first secret involves loving the people with whom one works. Although Fullan explains this secret with the administrator in mind, the school librarian should also remember this fact. School librarians have a group of teachers, coworkers, and administrators with whom they work. The school librarians must show they really enjoy working with these members of the learning community, treating everyone fairly and respecting teachers for the value they bring to the school. Fullan's second secret is the responsibility of assisting people in understanding their connection with the purpose of the project. Teachers need to see the value of working with the school librarian. Collaboration cannot be seen as an added duty but as a value-added process to help students learn. With all of the responsibilities of school librarians and teachers, collaboration is sometimes seen as more work and taking time away from other duties. Initially, this may be the case, but the end game of increased student learning must always be considered. As teachers and school librarians have success with a collaborative lesson, this "extra work" rationale will quickly disappear. Fullan's fifth secret is the need for transparency. Fullan uses this secret to discuss the need to share the data collected by organizations in a very open, clear, and understandable manner. This transparency will allow the organization to move forward with everyone traveling in the same direction. A school librarian can apply this principle to the change process by being open and honest with the processes and procedures used in the library. As the school librarian works with teachers in a collaborative manner, openness and willingness to share information is imperative. The school librarian and the school library program should be an "open book" to assure the teachers that changes made in the library program are to reach the goal of increased student learning. Teachers should understand the school librarian's vision of working collaboratively with them from the initial idea for the lesson to the final assessment. Understanding and applying these three secrets of the change process, as described by Fullan, will assist the school librarian in becoming a true instructional partner while affecting change.

BECOMING AN INSTRUCTIONAL PARTNER IN A NUTSHELL

The scene is a small elementary school. The players are the school librarian and the fourth-grade teachers. The place is a planning session for an upcoming lesson. The lead teacher reviews the unit plan from the last academic year. The teachers and school librarian discuss the changes that are needed. They then brainstorm about how this unit could be more effective with more students being engaged at a higher level. The school librarian identifies the need to provide additional work on the students' inquiry skills and also reviews additional resources that can be used in this process. The teachers and school librarian review the plan from the previous year and determine how to include more inquiry lessons. The planning team revises the schedule and divides up the tasks to be accomplished before meeting next week.

This example shows the results of a school librarian being an instructional partner. Prior to meetings like this, the school librarian followed these steps:

Studied the curriculum

Determined the resources that could be aligned with the curriculum

Developed relationships with the teachers

Began attending the planning meetings

Shared the vision of collaboration

Remembered that change is a slow process

Remembered that baby steps that bring small successes should be celebrated

As the school librarian follows these guidelines, he or she will participate in many of the just described planning meetings and experience successful collaborative encounters with the teachers. Each such encounter will continue to develop and enhance the school librarian's role as instructional partner.

WHAT DOES ALL OF THIS MEAN?

In this chapter we analyzed the role of instructional partner, reviewed the evolution of this role through the standards, and identified possible steps to follow to implement the changes necessary to establish this role. Evolving into an instructional partner can be a difficult task. School librarians must assess the culture of their schools, identify innovators or early adopters (Rogers 2003) willing to work with them to establish a collaborative role, and through transparency convince classroom teachers that partnership is a win/win event for all involved: teachers, administrators, school librarians, and students. Each of these steps take planning, reflection, and developing relationships with administrators and faculty members. If school librarians provide the transparency of their motives, and the passion for their professions, becoming an instructional partner will begin to evolve. Through successful collaborative encounters, this role as instructional partner will grow and flourish. This evolution will occur as school librarians exhibit their leadership abilities.

Reflective Questions

What does collaboration look like in my school?

What additional work do I need to do to create a collaborative culture in my school?

Which of my teachers are Innovators and which are Early Adopters (Rogers, 2003)?

How can I use the change process to become an instructional partner?

What is the first step I should take to establish my role as an Instructional Partner?

8

The Learning Community

After reading this chapter, school librarians will understand the concept of a learning community, its various configurations, and how to work with the different groups to establish a vibrant learning community in their workplace. Strategies for collaborating with members of the learning community will be discussed as well as methods for creating learning communities through professional development.

In the movie, *Apollo 13* (Howard & Grazer, 2006), the engineers at the Space Center needed to work together to create a "gadget" that would allow the astronauts to conduct repairs on their spacecraft so they could successfully reenter the earth's atmosphere. The dramatic scene occurs when the engineers dump all of the materials on a table that replicated the items available on the spacecraft that could be used to find a solution. And they did, by working together as members of their learning community. This concept of learning communities and working together is imperative for the role of the school librarian in the twenty-first century. In previous years, the role of school librarians has often been termed as one that could be very isolated (Hartzell, 1994, 2003). The teachers teach the students and the school librarians provide access to the materials. As we have noted, this concept of isolation has changed with the implementation of the recent standards for school librarians (AASL, 2009; AASL & AECT, 1998) and more emphasis has been placed on community building through learning communities. Different definitions and a variety of configurations of learning communities have evolved and it is important to understand these concepts.

The term learning community has many synonyms: global web of individuals and organizations (AASL & AECT, 1998); learning environment (AASL, 2009); a community of practice (Lave and Wenger, 1991; Wenger, 1998; Wenger, McDermott, and Snyder, 2002); Professional Learning Community (DuFour & Eaker, 1998; Hall & Hord, 2006); and Critical Friends Group (Bambino, 2002; National Reform Faculty, 2014) to name a few. Each of these definitions speaks to community and learning. Each has a different meaning and slightly different focus. Each impacts the field of education, and school librarians should under-stand their different parameters and roles in learning communities.

WHAT IS A LEARNING COMMUNITY?

This concept can be traced back to John Dewey (1859–1952) and Alexander Meiklejohn (1872–1964). The idea is also reminiscent of the higher education learning communities at Oxford, Cambridge, and other English universities (Fink & Inkelas, 2015).

John Dewey's (1938) philosophy of education included more than students attending classes and having facts presented and then completing tests on the material. He saw education as the union of facts gained through personal experiences and the interaction of others in society. Dewey's philosophy centered on democracy and society. He believed that the purpose of education was to assist students in becoming highly functional members of society. This transformation could take place through the marriage of traditional facts, personal experience, and interactions with other members of society. According to Harbour and Ebie (2011), Dewey established "Democratic Learning Communities" (p. 5) with this philosophy. With this alignment of experience and knowledge, Dewey visualized teachers and students engaged in a process of collaborative inquiry (Gabelnick, MacGregor, Matthews & Smith, 1990).

Another form of a learning community was the residential college model found in England and that was prevalent in the early years of higher education. This model provided sleeping residences, meals, and classes in one specific college. The students and professors formed a learning community and used the resources of the community to further their growth. Meikeljohn embraced the residential model for a learning community but believed that the college should be a unit unto itself and separated as much as possible from society (Fink & Inkelas, 2015).

Both of these configurations had people joining together to learn and accomplish their own goals. The most significant difference between the two is that Dewey described a successfully educated person as one who united with others to explore their own experiences as they related to their place in society, whereas Meikeljohn's learning communities were centered at institutions of higher education and, as much as possible, were removed from the general influences of society.

Today the term "learning community" is not confined to a specific higher education institution model nor is it the marriage of experience and societal influences. A learning community is a group of people who are connected because of goals and objectives and a wish to move their organization or group forward through collaboration and implementing cooperative projects. When using the term "learning community" in the world of education a variety of interpretations occur. The previous definition of learning community does hold true, but the focus is different when aligning it with the school librarians' roles as instructional partners and information specialists. The learning community concept can be seen through a position responsibility lens and through a school lens.

POSITION RESPONSIBILITY LENS

The Information Power Logo in the 1998 *Information Power: Building Partners for Learning* (AASL & AECT, 1998, p. 48) graphically depicted the roles of the school librarian and their relationships to the information literacy standards for student learning, teaching, information access, and program administration. The ring superimposed on this Venn diagram indicated this would be accomplished through leadership, technology, and collaboration. These concepts were infused throughout *Information Power*. Encircling these concepts was the term Learning Community surrounded by a circle of dashes with space in-between each dash. The interpretation of the space in-between the dashes was that the learning community encompassed the school and extended outside of the school building. Within the school the learning community included the principal, teachers, and staff members. The school librarian developed relationships with all members of the school community through collaboration and for the purpose of student learning. *Empowering Learners: Guidelines for School Library Programs* (AASL, 2009) exhorts school librarians to also develop these types of relationships with the school members. Both of these documents state it is the school librarians' role to push out from the confines of the school itself and to develop collaborative relationships with parents and organizations in the neighborhood.

What would this look like? One obvious connection with the community would be through the parents' group. School librarians might attend the monthly meetings and familiarize themselves with the parents and community members who attend the meetings. From there, collaborative partnerships could be formed that will enhance the students' learning in school. Public libraries and academic libraries are natural partners in a learning community. School librarians could reach out to their professional colleagues and develop collaborative groups to benefit the students and parents in the community. An often-overlooked connection for establishing collaborative relationships is with any business in the area. Technology entities should be on the list. How about movie theatres? A bookstore is another institution the school librarians could contact to develop a collaborative relationship and establish the infrastructure for a learning community.

As school librarians work with the faculty, administrators, and staff within the school and extend beyond the school walls to engage in collaborative activities with other organizations, they will be establishing collaborative relationships with common goals and the anticipation of increasing the learning opportunities for students. The world is growing ever smaller with immediate access to information. School librarians, as leaders, need to harness this information through the development of the learning community. This concept and definition of a learning community reflects the school librarians' role of working with the members of the learning community.

SCHOOL LENS

The concept of the learning community as described previously reflects the responsibility of the school librarian to work with a variety of entities through collaborative activities and with common goals that focus on learning.

Since the 1980s, educational entities themselves developed different learning communities that have specific structures (Gabelnick et al., 1990). Three of the most common configurations are: Community of Practice (CoP), Professional Learning Communities (PLC), and Critical Friends Groups (CFG). These learning communities are models addressing school improvement and change in individual schools and in school districts.

SCHOOL LENS: COMMUNITY OF PRACTICE

One type of learning community is called a community of practice. The concept of community of practice is not new, and Wenger, McDermott, and Snyder (2002) describe the early communities of practice as the first "knowledge-based social structures" (p. 5) existing historically at the time of the cavemen. Lave and Wenger (1991) formalized the term "community of practice" and discussed it in the context of an apprenticeship. People who work as apprentices are associated with the master teacher who assists the apprentice in learning a trade. Wenger, McDermott, and Snyder (2002) expanded this idea to include groups of people connected through a need to learn from each other about a particular idea. These groups can be found everywhere and the reason for the members of each group working together is varied. Members of a soccer team may form a community of practice; a group of faculty members revising curriculum may form a community of practice; members of a family along with their extended family members may also form a community of practice. Communities of practice are groups of people who have come together because of something they are passionate about, want to learn more about the topic, and want to gain new knowledge through their interactions with other people. The example at the beginning of this chapter about *Apollo 13* (Howard & Grazer, 2006) could describe a community of practice. Formalizing the concept of Community of Practice (CoP), Wenger, McDermott, and Snyder (2002) developed a model for a CoP. A CoP has the following: a specific domain, a group of people forming a community, and an identified practice. In a CoP, members share an interest in a specific topic or idea and this describes the domain. The community describes the people who are interested in the domain and therefore come together to help each other and to learn from each other. The practice refers to the members of the community being practitioners in the domain area. The identified components of a CoP are: the Domain, the Community, and the Practice. The **Domain** identified the content for the members and explains the issues. The **Community** describes the members of the CoP, allowing them to be in a group to develop trust and mutual respect. The **Practice** describes the common knowledge the members exhibit as they work together as a group. These three components describe a CoP. Lave and Wenger (1991) further conceptualized this process of learning as situated learning that reflects Dewey's philosophy (1938). People do not learn from facts being presented to them, but learn through their interactions in society. The CoP provides this vehicle for learning through interactions with others who are interested and passionate about a specific area of knowledge, a specific domain.

SCHOOL LENS: PROFESSIONAL LEARNING COMMUNITY

A Professional Learning Community (PLC) is another type of learning community. This model was established as a means of implementing change in schools and continuing with school improvement. Various authors have provided outlines for different models of PLCs (DuFour & Eaker, 1998; Hall & Hord, 2006). Each of these models emphasizes a means for the professional staff to work together to increase student achievement (Hall & Hord, 2006). Hord (1997 as found in Hall & Hord 2006) identified five dimensions found in professional learning communities: shared values and vision, collective learning and application, supportive and shared leadership, supportive conditions, and shared personal practice.

In 1998, partly in response to the failure of effective educational school reform, Richard DuFour and Robert Eaker published *Professional Learning Communities at Work: Best Practices for Enhancing Student Achievement*. The basic tenet of this work is that for schools to succeed, they must function as learning organizations in charge of their own future instead of adhering to the ineffective school reforms of the 1980s and 1990s (DuFour & Eaker, 1998). DuFour and Eaker identify the following six dimensions that guide their model of a professional learning community: a shared mission, vision, and values; collective inquiry; collaborative teams; action orientation and experimentation; continuous improvement; and results orientation.

Although configured in different ways, both of these models have similarities: shared missions and values, collaborative teams, and the presence of learning. Both models emphasize the involvement of principals and administrators to use the PLCs for implementing change and school improvement.

A PLC can be a collection of collaborative teams or the entire school depending on the purpose of the learning community. Some schools have PLCs comprised of grade level teachers or content specific teachers. Other collaborative teams revolve around a specific goal, a certain group of students that need help, or teachers from different schools that have a common interest or are working on a specific problem that affects all of them. DuFour and Marzano (2011) also suggest expanding the PLC through technology by virtually collaborating with colleagues. Schools have different configurations of PLCs with faculty members belonging to more than one collaborative group. A teacher could belong to a grade level PLC (team) where all members work together to create a learning environment for their grade level, and these same faculty members could individually belong to different PLCs organized for working with a specific group of students with similar learning needs (Howard, 2010a). PLCs are implemented to affect change and to improve student learning regardless of the configuration of the collaborative group. The necessary ingredients are collaboration, a shared vision, and a commitment to school improvement and change.

SCHOOL LENS: CRITICAL FRIENDS GROUP

Another type of learning community is a Critical Friends' Group (CFG). This type of community is focused more on a teacher's individual craft and

The Mountain Top CFG met on the second Tuesday of each week after school at the leader's home. This CFG included an art teacher, a music teacher, a history teacher, a school librarian, an assistant principal, an English teacher, a PE teacher, and a Spanish teacher. All of the participants are colleagues at Mountain Top High School. Each of the members is looking for assistance in creating lessons or revising them, so the lessons are more effective for their students. All of the members are committed to the school and want to make it even better for all of the faculty, students, and members of the learning community. The Mountain Top CFG has been in existence for one semester and during that time, the members have developed a sense of trust and acceptance for the diversity of its members.

At today's meeting, Ms. Sparks, an English teacher, is seeking comments on a lesson she has revised for the seniors in their Senior Seminar class. Using an agreed-upon Tuning Protocol, Ms. Sparks takes about 10 minutes to describe the revised lesson and presents it as the others listen. The group then takes 5 minutes to ask clarifying questions. The members of the group, except for Ms. Sparks, then take about 10 minutes to give warm and cool comments about the lesson. This is followed by a 10-minute general conversation, which includes Ms. Sparks. Ms. Sparks has taken notes during this process and will reflect on the suggestions, revise her lesson, and return for additional feedback at the next CFG meeting.

During the second half of the meeting, Mr. Dominic, the school librarian, describes a school-wide project he wishes to implement in the fall of the following year. The same Tuning Protocol is used to provide warm and cool feedback on this project. Mr. Dominic will also reflect on this information and return with revisions the following month.

Figure 8.1   Sample Critical Friends Group

the adoption of best practices for the teacher and the teacher's students. The Annenberg Institute of School Reform at Brown University developed CFGs in 1994 as a means of professional development for educators (National School Reform Faculty, 2014). Since 2000 the Critical Friends Group training has been conducted by the National School Reform Faculty (NSRF) at the Harmony Education Center in Bloomington, Indiana. A CFG is a learning community and could be classified as a PLC, but the focus is a bit different. CFGs are for professional improvement for the educator through a reflective group (Bambino, 2002, Cox, E. 2015). CFGs are focused more on the educator's craft and the improvement of that craft through the help and guidance of other members of the CFG. A typical CFG is comprised of 8 to 12 members and the members are connected with each other through their place of work. The only requirement for joining a CFG is the desire to improve one's practice and the commitment to meet with the group for one to two hours a month. This type of learning community also involves collaboration but employs evaluative protocols or structured interactions to work on best practices (see Figure 8.1).

Critical Friends Groups involve a great amount of trust and confidentiality among its members. At one of the first meetings of a CFG, specific norms are established to create this safe environment. This type of culture will allow members to develop their own craft through reflection while striving for excellence for themselves and their students (National School Reform Faculty, 2014).

Professional learning communities, communities of practice, and critical friends' groups are types of learning communities having common goals, collaborative structures, and the desire to advance student achievement and to affect change. Implementing learning communities, regardless of the configuration, has become one means of addressing school improvement in the educational field today. Learning communities provide an impetus for collaboration among administrators, teachers, and school librarians. Collaboration is a vehicle to use for establishing the school librarian as an instructional partner. As school librarians identify these different types of learning communities in their own schools, they must find ways to become members of these groups.

SCHOOL LIBRARIANS AND LEARNING COMMUNITIES

To assist in becoming members of learning communities, school librarians should reflect on two questions. Question 1: How do school librarians fulfill their responsibilities of developing relationships within their learning community? Question 2: How do school librarians work with existing learning communities that have developed in the school or should develop in the school?

Question 1: Developing Learning Community Relationships

To answer this question, school librarians should first identify the players inside the school. These players would include the principal and other administrators, teachers, and staff members. Members of the learning community outside the school, as mentioned earlier in this chapter, include the parents' group, information organizations such as public and academic libraries, and business organizations that can support the school's curriculum. Before the school librarians can determine how to proceed, they must reflect on the audience in the learning community. Figure 8.2 provides a list of possible questions that will help begin this reflection.

Armed with this information, the school librarian can now determine how to proceed and plan how to actively engage and work with members of the learning community. Many of the suggestions in earlier chapters should be revisited especially how to work with the faculty and staff in the curriculum area and how to develop a relationship with the principal. Using the information gathered from the environmental scans in Chapter 6, Collection Development, will provide a good overview of the different organizations available to collaborate with the school community. School librarians need to understand their audiences as they determine how to become members of learning communities.

Question 2: Existing School Learning Communities

The answer to this question has the school librarian taking a microscopic look at the learning communities already developed and functioning in the school. The first step in this process is also one of reflection. As school librarians consider the reflective questions in Figure 8.3, they may already have a good idea of what is

---

Principal and Administrative Staff
What is the leadership style of the principal?
How does this style align with my leadership style?
How can I support the principal and still fulfill my role as an Instructional Partner?
How do I convince the principal that I need administrative support and backing to assume this role?

Teachers and Staff Members
How do the teachers view the school librarian?
Which teachers are the leaders on the faculty?
Which teachers have the most influence on the faculty?
What are the curricular needs for the school?
How do I convince the teachers that I should be their instructional partner?
How do I explain to the other members of the staff what my responsibilities are?
How do I explain to all of them what the role of the school librarian should be regardless of what it has been in the past?

Organizations Outside of the School
What is the parent organization associated with the school?
Is this organization already working for the school?
Are there any other libraries in the geographic area associated with the school?
What is their relationship with my school?
Are there any businesses that I can contact that have a relationship with the school?
Are there any parents of our students that work for specific organizations that we can tap for helping with school resources?

Figure 8.2   Learning Community Reflective Questions

organized in the school. School librarians may not have had the opportunity in their school library training to witness being a member of a structured learning community so they should consider the questions in Figure 8.3.

As school librarians identify the learning communities already established, they must decide which groups are aligned with the goals of the school library and will provide the impetus to student learning. School librarians must consider the time factor and use their energy in the most effective way. Joining each existing group may be problematic and may not align with school librarians' other responsibilities. School librarians must be realistic in what can be accomplished productively. The guiding principle of less is more from the Coalition of Essential Schools (2016) applies to professional activities as well as curriculum units.

The school librarian may find there are pockets of collaboration occurring in different forms than have been presented here. The important concept is to determine the focus of the group to decide how to assist with its implementation and expansion to help with working as an instructional partner. As school librarians consider these questions, the culture and environment of the school will become clear, and they can reflect on how the school library program can improve by aligning with these groups. The school librarian should then take steps to meet with the members of the groups, maybe attend as an observer, and then gradually become a member. If school librarians are not able to identify or find any groups that are geared toward these types of collaboration, then they should decide what will be the most effective ways to create a collaborative

Are there any established learning communities in the school?
If the answer is yes, what is the configuration of this learning community?
Is there a PLC, a CFG or a CoP?
If a PLC, what is its function? Is it a grade level PLC? Or is it one with a different focus?
If it is a CoP, what is its function?
If it is a CFG, who are the members? What is their focus?
Who are the members of each of the established learning communities?
What is the best way to gain entrance into these learning communities?

Figure 8.3 Existing Learning Communities

environment through a learning community. They should discuss the concept of collaborative groups with their administrators to determine how to proceed. School librarians should then start small inviting members of the faculty to visit the library and discuss how they can work together. Through continued short meetings and discussion, the school librarian as a leader will be able to lay the groundwork for either a PLC, a CoP, or even a CFG. Each of these learning communities will achieve the goal of establishing a shared vision and an increase in student learning.

Once school librarians have established working with or establishing collaborative groups in the school community, then the attention should be turned to outside the school walls. Once again this is a gradual process. School librarians should contact the identified entities in the community and begin the conversation with them as to how all of them can help the students in the school. The initial contact may be through a phone call, an e-mail, or a visit with the sole purpose of introducing themselves and the school library program to the organization. Establishing these relationships may be a slow process, but one that will be an exciting one as the school librarian is pushing out the walls of the school and bringing the library program into the wider learning community.

PROFESSIONAL DEVELOPMENT

Once school librarians understand the concept of learning communities, both within the school and in the community outside the school, they need to determine how best to utilize the learning communities to fulfill their role as instructional partners. School librarians should consider their responsibility for professional development activities (AASL, 2009). The majority of these activities will be centered on interactions with the members of the faculty and the staff, and the methods of providing these trainings can take many forms (Abilock, Fontichiaro & Harada, 2012; Cox, M., 2015; Harvey, 2013; Joyce & Calhoun, 2010). The exciting part about working with professional development as a school librarian is that this can be accomplished with individuals, with a small group, through networking, and through presentations, either face-to-face or through electronic means. Each opportunity will provide a means for school librarians to illustrate their role as leaders and instructional partners. School librarians need to determine which method will work best for them. The first step is to determine the professional development (PD) needs of the staff. The following questions should be considered:

- Has the district implemented a new type of technology that the staff may need training to use effectively in their classrooms?
- Has the school librarian overheard staff members discussing a new software program they are interested in?
- Has the library acquired new resources that the staff should be aware of?

These types of questions need to be answered before any successful professional development is planned. The second step in implementing any professional development activities is to determine the best vehicle to use to present the information. The school librarian has determined the existence of collaborative groups in the building either as learning communities or loosely organized groups that naturally gravitate toward each other. These groups may be the means to present some of these professional development activities. The vehicle for the PD does not matter, but using an existing learning community will make the process easier. Collaboration and working together are essential to increase one's knowledge and skills to work with students.

WHAT DOES ALL OF THIS MEAN?

The concept of learning communities has been examined as a means of increasing learning for the students and staff. Three popular models of learning communities are: Communities of Practice (CoP), Professional Learning Communities (PLC), and Critical Friends Groups (CFG). All of them have similarities and the purpose of all of them is to implement change, continue with school improvement, and learn through collaborative groups. School librarians have the responsibility to use these types and other types of collaborative configurations to present relevant professional development to the administrators and staff. The twenty-first century is an age of collaboration using social media to connect with different groups. On a smaller scale, school librarians should use learning communities to collaborate with their colleagues and fulfill their roles as instructional partners, working hand in hand with teachers, administrators, and other members of the community.

Reflective Questions

Reflecting on Professional Learning Communities, Communities of Practice, and Critical Friends' Groups, which configuration will provide the best vehicle for you to use in collaborating with the members of your school community?

What learning communities are in existence in your school and how effective are they?

What steps will you take to become a member of a learning community already existing in your school?

What are the professional development needs of your staff?

How can you utilize a learning community to assist with your school's professional development needs?

Chapter 9

Teacher and School Librarian Partnership

At the end of this chapter, school librarians will understand the common categories of learning theories and how these theories impact the school library curriculum through the implementation of the Standards for the 21st-Century Learner *(AASL, 2007). The process of inquiry, the use of essential questions, and the integration of the process standards and content standards will be analyzed by identify best practices in the field. The role of the school librarian as instructional partner working with the classroom teacher will be reviewed.*

Chapter 8, The Learning Community, identified different configurations of groups working and collaborating together. In Chapter 9 the focus will be on the partnership between the teacher and the school librarian. Teachers know their curriculum and understand strategies for implementing that curriculum. School librarians know their curriculum and best practices for presenting that curriculum. The question is: How do these two entities work together to establish the collaborative partnership necessary for student learning?

LEARNING THEORIES

One facet of becoming a classroom teacher is studying educational theory. During this process students wade through many different ideas about education and how these ideas are implemented in schools. This information may not have seemed pertinent at the time, but when pre-service teachers become the gurus in the classroom, impacting 30 students for the entire day at the elementary level or 120 students during the day at the secondary level with the charge to "help students learn," the journey through the educational theories becomes more relevant. Educational theories are generally organized in three different categories: behaviorism, cognitivism, and constructivism.

Each of these philosophies has proponents who support the beliefs and have conducted research in their fields (Keesee, n.d.).

Behaviorism

The basic concept of this theory is that people learn through repeated acts. If a process is repeated a number of times, people will learn the concept. Learners are passive and simply wait for information and facts to be presented. If the facts are presented numerous times, learning will take place. One visual of this philosophy is that students sit quietly at their desks and the teacher opens up their heads and pours in facts. Students learn through practice and memorization of facts. Some behaviorists describe the mind as a black box waiting to be filled without any thought processes occurring in the mind (Nagowah & Nagowah, 2009). The information is simply poured in.

Cognitivism

Proponents of this philosophy believe that learners have more of a role and are not simply responding to stimuli. Supporters of cognitivism believe that when learners receive information, they have to process it to acquire knowledge. Cognitive theory revolves around how a person processes information. The facts are presented and cognitivists study how those facts are processed for the person to learn.

Constructivism

This theory considers the person's experience in the process of learning. It contends that the learner acquires knowledge through discovery, being presented with a problem to solve and relating the problem to prior experiences, and through experimentation to gain new knowledge. This theory echoes Dewey's (1938) role of experience; learners align their experiences with their problem-solving abilities and through this process gain new knowledge.

Supporters of these categories of learning theory form a continuum that span from one end of the spectrum to the other. Philosophers develop theories and then implement them based on their research and beliefs. The challenge for educators is to determine the best tenets of each philosophy to be used to help students learn. Each of these schools of thought has positive points to consider and each can be used effectively given the type of learning that needs to take place. In theory, all three philosophies can be used in some instances of learning. When learning how to drive a car, for example, the student should use the behaviorist theory to learn the specific driving rules: when to start, when to stop, and when to change lanes. Using the cognitive lens, the potential driver should understand the reasoning behind these rules, such as when it is safe to change lanes and why, or when it is safe to turn left and why. The actual experience of driving the car supports the constructivist theory as through practice the driver understands how to drive through doing. For effective learning to occur, portions of all three types of learning theories may be employed. Before collaborative lessons are successful, the school librarian and the classroom teacher need to determine the best methods to use to support the learning process for a specific lesson or unit. Additionally, the two need to work together to arrive at an agreement of which theory will guide the specific unit or lesson and their collaboration.

INQUIRY

One of the Common Beliefs in *Standards for the 21st-Century Learner* (AASL, 2007) identifies the framework of learning as inquiry. This concept is repeated in the standards themselves, using inquiry and critical thinking in Standard 1 and problem solving and creating new knowledge in Standard 2 (AASL, 2007). Inquiry supports the constructivist learning theory in helping students discover knowledge through activities that connect with their prior knowledge and answering thought-provoking questions. The process of inquiry was evident in the time of Socrates as his method of helping students learn was through posing questions that he did not answer, but that the students answered to provide them with deeper meaning and understanding. The inquiry method is certainly different from providing facts for the students to memorize. With inquiry, students combine their prior knowledge with what they are learning through their explorations. This concept of inquiry sets the direction for school librarians to follow when working with today's students. Inquiry is not a static process but an active one.

Stripling (2003) describes inquiry as a learning framework that allows students to begin with student-generated questions to investigate all resources to find the answer to those questions. The goal is to merge the student's personal knowledge and experience with this investigation to develop a new understanding within the student. To accomplish this, the student needs to be in the center of the investigation to follow where the resources lead. Stripling's inquiry framework includes six processes: students connect with their own previous knowledge (Connect); they develop questions (Wonder); they evaluate information to answer their questions (Investigate); they construct new understandings and draw conclusions (Construct); they express new ideas (Express) and they reflect on their findings by generating new questions (Reflect).

Inquiry is student-centered with student-developed research through questions they develop and need to have answered to increase their understanding and knowledge. The challenge of inquiry-based learning from the teachers' and school librarians' frame of reference is to develop lessons that will support the inquiry process and the curriculum and standards appropriate for the students' grade level. The content is found in the standards; the method is through inquiry. To align the standards through the inquiry process, the teachers and school librarians need to construct lessons around questions that will stimulate this atmosphere of inquiry.

Loertscher, Koechlin, and Zwaan (2005) address the need to develop inquiry-based questions that encourage educators to ban the bird units. Bird units are similar to state units, country units, and units on historical events that typically ask students for facts they can find through various search engines or through the use of an encyclopedia or other reference source. Students search the topic they are assigned, paraphrase or copy and paste the information into the required format, and then regurgitate the information to the teacher. Students may learn some facts from this but have really not used any higher-level thinking processes to evaluate the information or to determine if the information is correct. The information is just shared as it was found. Questions stimulating inquiry need to be ones that empower the students to think and make judgments about the information they find. For example, instead of asking students to complete a state report, students could compare the economic environment of two different states and provide a rationale for which state they would prefer to have as their residence complete with reasons why. This type of question will stimulate the students thinking and require them to use higher-level thinking skills found on Bloom's taxonomy of educational objectives (Bloom, 1956).

ESSENTIAL QUESTIONS

Much attention has been given to developing questions that will stimulate this inquiry. In 1984, Ted Sizer founded The Coalition of Essential Schools (CES) to address the restructuring of the American high school (Coalition of Essential Schools, 2016). The vision of CES is to prepare all students intellectually and emotionally, and to develop their social habits to become informed citizens. Ten principles guide CES to develop and implement a curriculum that will support this vision. The second principle, "Less is more: depth over coverage," encourages educators to expose students to concepts through in-depth exploration instead of providing students with myriad facts and events. This goal can be achieved through the use of the inquiry framework of learning. Essential questions are a tool that supports the implementation of the inquiry method.

What is an essential question? An essential question is a "big" question. It is an open-ended question that provides an opportunity to consider myriad possibilities to determine an answer. It requires research to look at different options; it causes students to think. Although researchers have described essential questions in different ways (Harada & Yoshina, 2004; Jacobs, 1997; McTighe & Wiggins 2013; Wiggins & McTighe 1998; Wiggins & McTighe, 2005), there are common characteristics identifying these types of questions. Jacobs (1997) identifies essential questions as ones that speak to the heart of what students need to know about a specific topic. These questions assist the student in understanding the basic content students will remember long after the lessons are finished. McTighe and Wiggins (2013) identify the following seven characteristics of essential questions: open-ended; thought-provoking and intellectually engaging; uses higher-order thinking; addresses important transferable ideas; raises additional questions; requires support and justification for any answer; and the question can and should be revisited (p. 3). Harada and Yoshina (2004) identify similar characteristics but state essential questions are abstract and address the essence of the content, leading to enduring truths the student will make part of their intellectual makeup. The common characteristics of these models are: using open-ended questions,

Table 9.1   Common Characteristics of Essential Questions

Common Characteristics of Essential Questions Based on Harada and Yoshina's (2004) model and McTighe and Wiggins's (2013) model
Open-ended
Thought-provoking, addresses the essence of the content
Uses higher-order thinking skills
Stimulates additional questions
Becomes part of the students' core beliefs, the concepts and values that remain with them after the lesson is completed.

addressing important ideas, and stimulating further questions for additional study (see Table 9.1). Teachers spend much of the day asking questions and expecting answers. But the questions many times require the student to provide only a fact without much thinking. Using essential questions will provide the opportunity for students to use higher-level thinking skills, those on the upper levels of Bloom's taxonomy: analysis, synthesis, and evaluation (Bloom, 1956).

As the school librarian and classroom teachers develop curriculum, they must create essential questions at the unit level and the lesson level to stimulate the process of inquiry. Developing essential questions is a skill and is an effective way to work with students through inquiry. The essential questions listed in Table 9.2 can guide units that support content standards or specific lessons within units.

The examples in Table 9.2 are essential questions to stimulate the student's thinking. None of these questions can be answered with a simple yes or no; they will require the students to think, research, reflect on their own experiences and come to some definite conclusions. In other words, they will need to use the learning frame of inquiry to answer these questions. As the essential questions are presented to the students, they can then use Stripling's (2003) Inquiry Process noted previously to answer the questions.

The essential questions in Table 9.2 address specific content standards found in the curriculum. Teachers plan activities addressing the content standards reflected in these questions. How does the school librarian fit in? How does the classroom teacher need to partner with the school librarian?

Table 9.2   Sample Essential Questions

How has the United States' immigration policy affected the culture of America? (History)
How did the Vietnam War affect the American's value system? (History)
How can obesity be eliminated? (Health/PE)
What makes a fictional story a classic? (English)

SCHOOL LIBRARY CURRICULUM

Teachers have the content of their disciplines as the basis for their curriculum, and this content is explained through the state standards. The content of the school library program is information. How does one seek, find, evaluate, and organize information? And how does one create knowledge as a result of seeking this information? The answers to these questions explain the school library curriculum. In *Information Power: Building Partnerships for Learning* (1998), this curriculum was described through the information literacy standards. *Information Power* listed the nine information literacy standards, provided indicators for each standard, and identified the levels of proficiency. The Information Literacy standards were also aligned with the content standards. This information provided a blueprint that enabled the school librarians to provide the tools for the students to become information literate. When the *Standards for the 21st-Century Learner* (AASL, 2007) were adopted, the focus became the process of learning through inquiry. Each of the four standards includes the skills, dispositions, responsibilities, and self-assessment strategies. These standards have the learner as the focus and address what the learner needs to know along with the criteria that can be used to enhance this learning. Inquiry is key and this is reflected in the standards.

Empowering Learners, Guidelines for School Library Programs (AASL, 2009) shifts the focus of the standards. Four guidelines are given addressing the following ideas: Collaboration, Reading, Multiple Literacies, Inquiry, and Assessment (p. 19). Having collaboration as the first guideline is no accident. Collaboration among teachers, school librarians, and administrators is pivotal in helping students learn and in establishing an effective school library program (Howard, 2010a). Collaboration is the way the school librarian will establish a partnership with the classroom teacher, and together they will develop the inquiry-based units to stimulate student learning.

The school librarian should prepare for the collaborative partnership with the classroom teacher by determining the research process that is best to use at the school. Many research models are available (Eisenberg & Berkowitz 1990; Kuhlthau, 2004; Stripling & Pitts, 1998, Tallman & Joyce, 2006). Each of these models leads the student through the process of addressing the essential question for the unit or for the lesson. Callison and Preddy (2006) identify five elements involved with research models: Questioning, Exploration, Assimilation, Inference, and Reflection. These research models address the following five elements.

Questioning: The research model should include the act of questioning. The question may be developed through the essential question of the unit or the lesson, or it may emanate from the curiosity of the student.

Exploration: This process may occur before an actual question develops or evolves from analyzing the question. The two go hand-in-hand. The students may begin with the knowledge they already have using a graphic organizer such as a K-W-L chart where the students register what they know about the topic, what they wish to know and then, after exploration, what they have learned about the topic (Harada & Yoshina, 2004).

Assimilation: This is the act of absorbing what the students have learned and coincides with the exploration phase of research.

Inference: Inference addresses the conclusions that students develop based on the other phases of their inquiry.

Reflection: This provides an opportunity for students to evaluate if they have answered their questions and to determine if other questions have emanated from their research.

Research models used for inquiry have these different levels of processing information but may go by other names. Using these categories as guides, school librarians should explore different research models and determine which one best fits with the culture of their schools and the teaching styles of the educators in their schools. Once school librarians have determined a workable research model, they should then prepare for partnering with the classroom teachers.

PARTNERSHIP ROLE

In Chapter 7, Instructional Partner and Change, the school librarian's role of instructional partner was analyzed through the lens of change, identifying the different categories of people and how they are willing to accept change (Rogers, 2003). These categories need to be reviewed as classroom teachers will be on a continuum as to accepting the school librarian as a partner. Some teachers may still see the school librarian as a person who provides the resources but not necessarily as a partner. In Chapter 7, a list of prior activities for the school librarian before addressing the possibility of a partnership was also offered. This list can be expanded to include:

- State and National standards
- Implementation of a Research Model
- Individual Relationships

State and National Standards

In addition to reviewing the curriculum of the school, the school librarian should reflect on how these content standards address the inquiry process. Is there a statement in the standards requiring the students to use higher-level thinking skills through an inquiry process? What essential question could be developed to achieve this standard? What could be the school librarian's role in helping the students use the inquiry process to answer the question? In other words, school librarians need to reflect on how they would accomplish this standard IF they were a classroom teacher. It will then be an easy step to align this with the research process.

Implementation of a Research Model

Which Research Model will work best with the teachers in the school? This may be a hard question but one that must be considered. School librarians should analyze the ones referred to previously, or any other appropriate research model, and make certain this model looks like it will "fit" with the school. Then the school librarian can begin discussing this with members of the faculty just in general terms to see if there is interest or a willingness to use this research model. If the school is already using a specific model, the school librarian needs to analyze the positive points about the model already in place. Sometimes, it is better to continue with what the teachers are already familiar with before implementing a major change. If there is no model in place, then the school librarian should continue discussing a possible new model.

Individual Relationships

This step is the hardest and is where the school librarian really illustrates the role of being a leader. This entails establishing relationships with the classroom teachers as mentioned in Chapter 7, Instructional Partner and Change, but also includes meeting with individual teachers to establish more individualized relationships. Here the school librarian needs to review the different leadership styles presented in Chapter 2, Curriculum Leadership, and try to determine what course of action to follow with the individual teacher. What is the teacher's leadership style? Is the teacher someone who is assertive and wants to be in control of any planning? Would he or she rather discuss the big picture and not want to worry about the details of the lesson or the process to be used in planning? "It will all just come together." Is the teacher concerned that everyone is comfortable with the planning process and may be so receptive to other's ideas that the school librarian may not understand what the teacher is really thinking? Or does the person need to plan every detail of the lesson to the extent that the time factor in collaborating is astronomical? These are four different types of learning styles based on a compass style tuning protocol developed by the National School Reform Faculty (2014).

- What type of learning style does Ms. White have?
- How should I work with her?
- What information does she need for us to begin forming a partnership?

These are the types of questions that the school librarian should consider as plans are made to develop the role of instructional partner. "It takes two to tango," a popular idiom in the English language, maps out the strategy for the school librarian. A person can't become a partner without the other person's willingness to participate in the relationship. The more reflection, planning, and study that the school librarian is able to accomplish will become a barometer for establishing a successful instructional partnership. The goal for the school librarian is to develop as many of these partnerships as possible, so that the process of inquiry will spread throughout the school. Students, teachers, and other members of the learning community will be the ones who profit by these partnerships.

WHAT DOES ALL OF THIS MEAN?

This chapter provided an overview of learning theory and the different types that should be considered while planning lessons. In addition, the chapter examined the concept of inquiry and its role in student learning. The concept of inquiry is far different than having the students provide facts about a certain topic. Inquiry is challenging the students to exercise their higher- level thinking skills. Inquiry requires students to "think." By working with classroom teachers on units and lessons, and developing essential questions that will stimulate the students, inquiry will be accomplished. School librarians should work with their classroom teachers to select or develop a research model that will ensure that students participate in inquiry research. This task could be considered daunting but is achievable.

Reflective Questions

What type of learning philosophy is prevalent in my school? Is it the most effective one to use with our students?

What does inquiry look like in my teachers' classrooms? Is it vibrant?

What inquiry research model will be the most effective one to use with our students?

What steps should I implement to establish an instructional partnership with my most difficult teacher?

Chapter 10

Beyond the School

This chapter will provide information on how a school librarian can continue the role of instructional partner through opportunities at the district, state, and national levels. Possible strategies for fulfilling this role will be offered.

Empowering Learners: Guidelines for the School Library Program (AASL, 2009) added the role of Leader to the existing roles for the school librarian. In Chapter 2, What is Curriculum Leadership, this leadership concept was analyzed and aligned with the school librarian's curriculum responsibilities. Much of the focus to this point has been on the leadership role in the school and in the local community. Leadership does not end there and the school librarian has the responsibility to explore ways to impact student learning as an instructional partner at the local, district, state, and national levels.

LOCAL ORGANIZATIONS

Chapter 8, The Learning Community, describes the school librarian pushing out from the school structure itself and making connections and forming collaborative groups with organizations such as the public library, the parent's group, and similar organizations supporting student learning. School librarians should review their environmental scan developed as they constructed their collection map to determine other organizations where normal partnerships could be formed. Then the school librarian should take the initiative to contact these organizations and begin developing a partnership with them. Working with these organizations will provide a cornucopia of learning activities to engage the students.

One of the common partnerships for the school librarian is with the public library, and through this partnership the school librarian extends the role of instructional partner to include collaborating with the public librarians. This collaborative partnership could involve developing units on literacy or units on digital literacy. The school librarian and the public librarian would plan literacy activities working with students at either the school or the public library to

Table 10.1   Additional Leadership Opportunities

Local Organizations Found in the school's learning community	District Committees assigned by the school library director	State Professional Library Association	National and International
International Reading Association—local chapter	Curriculum committees for content areas	American Association of School Librarians (AASL)	American Library Association (ALA)
International Society for Technology in Education (ISTE)—local chapter	Policy committee	International Reading Association—state chapter	International Federation of Library Association and Institutions
Public, academic, and special libraries based in the learning community	Materials Reconsideration Committee	Freedom to Read —state chapter	Freedom to Read National Organization
Local organizations in content areas such as math, science, and literacy organizations	Professional Development Committees	International Literacy Association	National organizations in specific content areas

increase their literacy knowledge. One common collaboration is through the summer reading program.

Additional possibilities include partnerships with the local division of the International Reading Association (IRA) and the International Society for Technology in Education (ISTE). The school librarian's role as instructional partner through leadership extends to all of these organizations. The school librarian needs to reflect on which organizations will provide the opportunities to enhance learning activities for the students. During this reflection the school librarians should consider the content areas of their educational backgrounds. If they have a background in science or math, they should determine if there are any organizations they could contact to discuss ways to develop learning activities. Regardless of their backgrounds, they should look for any literacy, reading, science, math, or historical organization as possible partners. These types of organizations present natural entities for curriculum partnerships. Table 10.1 lists possible local connections the school librarian should consider contacting.

DISTRICT

The previous iterations of the school library standards have encouraged school librarians to work closely with the district level supervisors to promote and support the school library program (ALA & AECT, 1975; AASL & AECT, 1988; AASL & AECT, 1998; AASL, 2009). The district library director will organize all facets of the school library program and support the school librarian's endeavors to increase student achievement. In a survey conducted in 2012 through the Lilead Project funded through the Institute of Museum and Library services (IMLS), school library supervisors listed a variety of ways they supported the school level librarian (Traska, 2014). These items included responsibilities for professional development at the building level, technology support, collection development guidance, alignment of content and information literacy standards, and advocacy for the school library program. The district level supervisors work closely with the school librarians to develop a learning community with the goal of establishing an effective school library program in each school and throughout the district. The methods of accomplishing this are different in each district and are dependent on the leadership style and the culture of the school district.

The leadership possibilities for school librarians supporting the district program are numerous and the district supervisor will need input on curriculum, schedules, standards, funding, and professional development topics. When the director indicates there is a need for volunteers, the school librarians should volunteer for these types of committees. The school library program is not in a cocoon and, many times, these committees will include educators from other disciplines. To talk about literacy without including the literacy department would be wasted effort. The school librarians should follow the lead of the supervisors while providing input based on their own experiences.

Some districts do not have a school library director. The school librarians may be supervised by the educational technology director or the literacy director. Sometimes the director of curriculum supervises the school librarians. In these situations, the school level librarians must assume the responsibility for increasing the level of knowledge for the directors from other disciplines. The school librarians must establish a comfortable working relationship with the directors and keep them abreast of the library landscape, including the highlights and the challenges.

Working with the director responsible for the school librarians is a natural fit. Other district opportunities for leadership are also available for the school librarian. The curriculum in each of the disciplines is continually being updated. School librarians would be a welcome addition to any of these district curriculum committees and could use these opportunities to discuss the research inquiry process. The district policy committee is an important leadership committee and many districts have educators as members of this type of committee. Policy committees review the policies and procedures that guide the school district. In addition, the policy committee reviews and approves the curriculum of the school district. Often this committee is responsible for challenges or reconsideration of materials used in the schools. School librarians have expertise in the intellectual freedom area and the district would profit by having such a knowledgeable member on this committee. These are just a few ideas of how the school librarian could function in the leadership role at the district level.

Smaller school districts may not have a person designated at the district level to supervise the school librarians and the responsibility for this falls to the principals of each school. School librarians in the district need to organize themselves through a collaborative learning community and, as a group or with a designated spokesperson, work with principals, administrators, and superintendents to illustrate the need for support in the school library field. This provides an incredible opportunity to establish one as a leader in the district, always remembering that any support at the district level will be support for the students in the school district. These administrators should understand that the school librarians are curriculum partners with the teachers. Table 10.1 lists possible district connections.

STATE, NATIONAL, AND INTERNATIONAL OPPORTUNITIES

As school librarians understand their leadership roles, they should extend their level of involvement to the state, national, and international areas. At the state level, the school librarian has opportunities to join the affiliate of the American Association of School Librarians (AASL). Some states have separate organizations for school libraries. Some states have all information professionals: school, public, academic, and special represented in one organization. School librarians should determine the organizational structure for their state and how they can become involved. Other organizations are represented at the state level also, and school librarians can determine which of these would be appropriate for increasing their leadership influence.

AASL is a division of the American Library Association (ALA) and being a member provides opportunities to help set the future direction for the association. The members of AASL make up the organization and each member has a right and a responsibility to move the organization forward to support its mission: "The American Association of School Librarians empowers leaders to transform teaching and learning" (AASL, 2016).

The American Library Association (ALA) is the parent organization and provides opportunities for all information professionals to be involved at the national level. When school librarians decide to reach out at the national level, this is the organization they should explore. Their website: www.ala.org provides valuable information concerning all facets of the information profession and how to become involved. The website also identifies the professional development opportunities available and continues to update its members on a daily basis.

The International Federation of Library Associations and Institutions (IFLA) expands the boundaries of the learning community and connects the school librarian with other information professionals on a global level. The mission of IFLA is to be a global voice for all information professionals. IFLA's website: http://www.ifla.org/ provides similar information that the ALA website does but with a global focus. Table 10.1 lists connections at the state, national, and international levels.

WHAT DOES ALL OF THIS MEAN?

These opportunities at the state, national, and international levels are avail-able when the school librarian is ready to take advantage of them. As a new school librarian, the opportunities at the district and local levels will provide an effective way to develop the instructional partner leadership role. When the school librarian is comfortable in these areas, it will then be time to explore the state, national, and international levels. The mantra of the school librarian as stated previously is that "baby steps" are the recipe for success. A plethora of opportunities are available at all levels and school librarians could become overwhelmed with how they should accomplish their leadership role. Challenges must be addressed and successes must be celebrated for school librarians to become effective leaders in the information field.

Reflective Questions

Which organizations in my local community are possible partners for our school? How should we work with them?

Which committees will be most conducive to my becoming an effective instructional partner?

When I am ready to expand my horizons, which level (state, national, or international) should I explore first and why?

A Final Word

As school librarians we are embarking on a profession that has information as a commodity. We are information professionals responsible for helping administrators, faculty, staff, and students find, access, and explore as much information as possible in all formats to increase and stimulate the intellectual ability needed to become well developed and thinking members of society. The curriculum of the school is a vehicle we use to accomplish this goal. Accessing information and understanding it leads to knowledge. Knowledge is imperative for intellectual development. This concept is an exciting idea related to the role of the information specialist and the instructional partner, both identified by the American Association of School Librarians (2009) as roles we must embrace. These roles can be accomplished through developing our leadership prowess, collaborating with teachers, and developing and implementing curriculum. The chapters in this book present guidelines and a road map to help us on this journey. If we embrace this profession and its responsibilities, our students and other members of the learning community will reap the benefits.

References

Abilock, Debbie, Kristin Fontichiaro, and Violet H. Harada. Eds. *Growing Schools: Librarians as Professional Developers.* Denver, CO: Libraries Unlimited, 2012.

American Association of School Librarians (AASL). "AASL: Mission Statement," www.ala.org/aasl/about (Cited May 26, 2016).

American Association of School Librarians (AASL). *Empowering Learners: Guidelines for School Library Programs.* Chicago, IL: American Association of School Librarians, 2009.

American Association of School Librarians (AASL). *Standards for the 21st-Century Learner.* Chicago, IL: American Association of School Librarians, 2007.

American Association of School Librarians (AASL) & Association of Educational Communications and Technology (AECT). *Information Power: Building Partnerships for Learning.* Chicago, IL: American Library Association (ALA) and Association for Educational Communications and Technology (AECT), 1998.

American Association of School Librarians (AASL) & Association of Educational Communications and Technology (AECT). *Information Power: Guidelines for School Library Media Programs.* Chicago, IL: American Library Association (ALA) and Association for Educational Communications and Technology (AECT), 1988.

American Association of School Librarians (AASL) & Association of Educational Communications and Technology (AECT). *Media Programs: District and School.* Chicago, IL: American Library Association (ALA) and Association for Educational Communications and Technology (AECT), 1975.

Argyris, Chris, and Donald A. Schon. *Organizational Learning: A Theory of Action Perspective.* Menlo Park, CA: Addison-Wesley Publishing Company, 1978.

Bambino, Deborah. "Critical Friends." *Educational Leadership* (March 2002): 25–27.

Bankhead, Betty. "Colorado Power Libraries Project the Answer Is Simple: Learn from the Best." *Colorado Libraries* 29 (2003): 12–14.

Bart, Ronald S. "Culture in Question." In *The Jossey-Bass Reader on Education Leadership.* 2nd ed., 159–168. San Francisco, CA: John Wiley & Sons, Inc. 2007.

Barton, Paul E. *National Education Standards: Getting Beneath the Surface.* Princeton, NJ: Educational Testing Service, 2009.

Bass, Bernard M. *Leadership and Performance Beyond Expectations.* New York, NY: Free Press, 1985.

Bass, Bernard M., and Ruth Bass. *The Bass Handbook of Leadership: Theory, Research, and Managerial Applications.* 4th ed. New York, NY: Free Press, 2008.

Beauchamp, George A. *Curriculum Theory.* 3rd ed. Wilmette, IL: The Kagg Press, 1975.

Bennis, Warren. *On Becoming a Leader.* New York, NY: Basic Books, 2003.

Bennis, Warren. *On Becoming a Leader.* New York, NY: Basic Books, 2009.

Bennis, Warren, and Burton Nanus. *Leaders: Strategies for Taking Charge.* 2nd ed. New York: HarperBusiness Essentials, 2003.

Bhargava, Rohit. "The 5 Models of Content Curation. Influential Marketing Blog." (Web Log Comment.) 2011. Retrieved from: http://www.rohitbhargava .com/2011/03/the-5-models-of-content-curation.html.

Bishop, Kay. *The Collection Program in Schools: Concepts and Practices.* 5th ed. Denver, CO: Libraries Unlimited, 2013.

Bloom, Benjamin S. *Taxonomy of Educational Objectives: The Classification of Educational Goals.* Handbook I: Cognitive Domain. New York, NY: David McKay, 1956.

Bolden, Richard, Jonathan Gosling, A. Marturano, and P. Dennison. *A Review of Leadership Theory and Competency Frameworks. Centre for Leadership Studies.* United Kingdom: University of Exeter, 2003.

Bolman, Lee G., and Terrence E. Deal. *Reframing Organizations: Artistry, Choice, and Leadership.* 5th ed. San Francisco, CA: Jossey-Bass, Inc., 2008.

Bradley, L. H. *Curriculum Leadership: Beyond Boilerplate Standards.* Lanham, MA: Scarecrow Education, 2004.

Brown, F. William, and Michael D. Reilly. "The Myers-Briggs Type Indicator and Transformational Leadership." *Journal of Management Development* 28 (2009): 916–932.

Brymer, Eric, and Tonia Gray. "Effective Leadership: Transformational or Transactional?" *Australian Journal of Outdoor Education* 10 (2006): 13–19.

Bucher, Holli. "Dewey vs Genre Throwdown." *Knowledge Quest* 42 (2013): 48–55.

Burns, James MacGregor. *Leadership.* New York, NY: Perennial, An Imprint of HarperCollins Publishers, 1978.

Callison, Daniel, and Leslie Preddy. *The Blue Book on Information Age Inquiry, Instruction and Literacy.* Westport, CT: Libraries Unlimited, 2006.

Carver, Kathleen W. "The Changing Instructional Role of the High School Library Media Specialist, 1950–84: A Survey of Professional Literature, Standards and Research Studies." *School Library Media Quarterly* 14 (1986): n.p.

Chemers, Martin M. *An Integrative Theory of Leadership.* Mahwah, NJ: Lawrence Erlbaum Associate, Publishers, 1997.

Coalition of Essential Schools (2016). Retrieved from http://essentialschools.org/.

Collins, Jim. *Good to Great: Why Some Companies Make the Leap and Others Don't.* New York, NY: HarperBusiness, 2001.

Collins, Suzanne. *The Hunger Games.* New York, NY: Scholastic, Inc., 2008.

Cookson, Peter W. "The Challenge of Isolation." *www.teachingk-8.com* (2005): 14–16.

Copeland, Michael A. "Leadership of Inquiry: Building and Sustaining Capacity for School Improvement." *Educational Evaluation and Policy Analysis* 25 (2003): 375–395.

Covey, Stephen R. *The 8th Habit: From Effectiveness to Greatness.* New York, NY: Free Press, A Division of Simon & Schuster, Inc., 2004.

Cox, Ernie. "Critical Friend's Groups: Learning Experiences for Teachers." *School Library Monthly* 27 (2015): 32–34.

Cox, Marge. "Back to the Future: Professional Development." *Knowledge Quest* 43 (2015): 46–52.

Deal, Terrence, and Kent D. Peterson. *Shaping School Culture: Pitfalls, Paradoxes, & Promises.* 2nd ed. San Francisco, CA: Jossey-Bass, Inc., 2009.

Dewey, John. *Experience and Education.* New York, NY: Collier Books, The Kappa Delta Pi Lecture Series, 1938.

Doll, Carol, and Pamela Petrick Barron. *Managing and Analyzing Your Collection: A Practical Guide for Small Libraries and School Media Centers.* Chicago, IL: American Library Association, 2002.

DuFour, Richard, and Robert Eaker. *Professional Learning Communities at Work: Best Practices for Enhancing Student Achievement.* Alexandria, VA: Association for Supervision and Curriculum Development (ASCD), 1998.

DuFour, Richard, and Robert J. Marzano. *Leaders of Learning: How District, School and Classroom Leaders Improve Student Achievement.* Bloomington, IN: Solution Tree, 2011.

Eisenberg, Michael B., and Robert E. Berkowitz. *Curriculum Initiative: An Agenda and Strategy for Library Media Programs.* Norwood, NJ: Ablex Publishing Corporation, 1988.

Eisenberg, Michael B., and Robert E. Berkowitz. *Information Problem-Solving: The Big Six Skills Approach to Library and Information Skills Instruction.* Worthington, OH: Linworth Publishing, 1990.

Evans, G. Edward, and Margaret Zamosky Saponaro. *Developing Library and Information Center Collections.* 5th ed. Westport, CT: Libraries Unlimited, 2005.

Fink, John E., and Karen Kurotsuchi Inkelas. "A History of Learning Communities within American Higher Education." *New Directions for Student Services* 149 (2015): 5–15.

Fullan, Michael. *Change Forces: Probing the Depths of Educational Reform.* New York, NY: The Falmer Press, 1993.

Fullan, Michael. *The Six Secrets of Change: What the Best Leaders Do to Help Their Organizations Survive and Thrive.* San Francisco, CA: Jossey-Bass, 2008.

Gabelnick, Faith, Jean MacGregor, Roberta S. Matthews, and Barbara Leigh Smith. "Learning Communities: Creating Connections among Students, Faculty and Disciplines." *New Directions for Teaching and Learning*, 41. San Francisco, CA: Jossey-Bass Inc., Publishers, 1990.

Geertz, Clifford. *The Interpretations of Cultures: Selected Essays.* New York, NY: Basic Books, 1973.

Glatthorn, Allan A., Floyd Boschee, and Bruce M. Whitehead. *Curriculum Leadership: Strategies for Development and Implementation.* 2nd ed. Los Angeles, CA: Sage Publications, 2009.

Gregory, Vicki L. *Collection Development and Management for 21st Century Library Collections: An Introduction.* New York, NY: Neal-Schuman Publishers, 2011.

Grover, Robert. *Collaboration: Lessons Learned.* Chicago, IL: American Association of School Librarians, 1996.

Hall, Gene E. and Sally M. Hord. *Implementing Change: Patterns, Principles, and Potholes.* 2nd ed. New York, NY: Pearson, 2006.

Hallinger, Philip, and Kenneth Leithwood. "Unseen Forces: The Impact of Social Culture on School Leadership." *Peabody Journal of Education* 73 (1998): 126–151.

Hamilton, David, M. Gibbons, and E. J. Brill. *Notes on the Origins of Educational Terms Class and Curriculum*. Paper presented at the annual convention of the American Educational Research Association (AERA), Boston, MA: April 7–11, 1980.

Harada, Violet H., and Joan Yoshina. *Inquiry Learning through Librarian-teacher Partnerships*. Worthington, OH: Linworth Publishing, Inc., 2004.

Harbour, Clifford P., and Gwyn Ebie. "Deweyan Democratic Learning Communities and Student Marginalization." *New Directions for Student Services* 155 (2011): 5–14.

Hargreaves, David H. "School Culture, School Effectiveness and School Improvement." *School Effectiveness and School Improvement* 6 (1995): 23–46.

Hartzell, Gary N. *Building Influence for the School Librarian*. Worthington, OH: Linworth Publishing, Inc., 1994.

Hartzell, Gary N. *Building Influence for the School Librarian: Tenets, Targets & Tactics*. 2nd ed. Worthington, OH: Linworth Publishing, Inc., 2003.

Harvey, Carl A. "Putting on the Professional Development Hat." *School Library Monthly* 29 (2013): 32–34.

Hatch, Mary Jo. *Organization Theory: Modern, Symbolic, and Postmodern Perspectives*. New York: Oxford University Press, 1997.

Haycock, Carol Ann. "The Changing Role: From Theory to Reality." In *School Library Media Annual*, edited J.B. Smith and J. G. Coleman, 61–67. Englewood, CO: Libraries Unlimited, 1991.

Henri, James. "Understanding the Information Literate School Community." In *Leadership Issues in the Information Literate School Community*, edited by James Henri and Marlene Asselin, 11–37. Westport, CT: Libraries Unlimited, 2005.

Hofstede, Geert, and Gert Jan Hofstede. *Cultures and Organizations: Software of the Mind*. San Francisco, CA: McGraw-Hill, 2005.

Howard, Jody K. "Basic Selection Tools: 21st-Century Style." *School Library Monthly* (2011): 9–11.

Howard, Jody K. "The Relationship between School Culture and the School Library Program: Four Case Studies." *School Library Research* 13 (2010a). Retrieved from: http://www.ala.org/aasl/sites/ala.org.aasl/files/content/aaslpubsandjournals/slr/vol13/SLR_RelationshipBetween.pdf.

Howard, Jody K. "Teacher-Librarian as a Curriculum Leader." In *The Many Faces of School Library Leadership*, edited by Sharon Coatney, 85–100. Santa Barbara, CA: ABC-CLIO, LLC, 2010b.

Howard, Ron and Brian Grazer. *Apollo 13*. [Motion Picture.] USA: Universal Studios, 2006.

Howell, Jane M., and Bruce J. Avolio. "Transformational Leadership, Transactional Leadership, Locus of Control, and Support for Innovation: Key Predictors of Consolidated-Business-Unit Performance." *Journal of Applied Psychology* 78 (1993): 891–902.

Institute of Education Sciences (IES). National Center for Education Statistics (NCES). Washington, D.C.: United States Department of Education. 2015. Retrieved from: https://nces.ed.gov/.

International Society for Technology in Education. 2016. Retrieved from: http://www.iste.org/STANDARDS.

Jacobs, Heidi H. *Getting Results with Curriculum Mapping*. Alexandria, VA: Association for Supervision and Curriculum Development (ASCD), 1997.

Jacobs, Heidi H. "A New Essential Curriculum for a New Time." In *Curriculum 21: Essential Education for a Changing World*, edited by Heidi H. Jacobs, 7–17.

Alexandria, VA: Association for Supervision and Curriculum Development (ASCD), 2010.

Johnson, Peggy. *Fundamentals of Collection Development and Management*. 2nd ed. Chicago, IL: American Library Association (ALA), 2009.

Joyce, Bruce, and Emily Calhoun. *Models of Professional Development: A Celebration of Educators*. Thousand Oaks, CA: Corwin, 2010.

Keesee, Gayla S. *Learning Theories*. n.d. Retrieved from: http://teachinglearning resources.pbworks.com/w/page/19919565/Learning%20Theories.

Kennedy, Ryan B., and D. Ashley Kennedy. "Using the Myers-Briggs Type Indicator in Career Counseling." *Journal of Employment Counseling* 4 (2004): 38–44.

Kilburg, Richard R., and Marc D. Donohue. "Toward a Grand Unifying Theory of Leadership." *Consulting Psychology Journal: Practice and Research* 63 (2011): 6–25.

Kimmel, Sue C. *Developing Collections to Empower Learners*. Chicago, IL: American Association of School Librarians, 2014.

Kouzes, Jim M., and Barry Z. Posner. *The Leadership Challenge*. 3rd ed. San Francisco, CA: Josey-Bass, 2002.

Kouzes, Jim M., and Barry Z. Posner. *Leadership Practices Inventory (LPI): Participant's Workbook*. Revised 2nd ed. San Francisco, CA: Jossey-Bass, 2009.

Kruse, Sharon D., and Karen S. Louis. *Building Strong School Cultures: A Guide to Leading Change*. Thousand Oaks, CA: Corwin Press, 2009.

Kuhlthau, Carol C. *Seeking Meaning: A Process Approach to Library and Information Services*. 2nd ed. Westport, CT: Libraries Unlimited, 2004.

Larson, Janette. *CREW: A Weeding Manual for Modern Libraries*. Austin, TX: Texas State Library and Archives Commission. 2012.

Lave, Jean, and Etienne Wenger. *Situated Learning: Legitimate Peripheral Participation*. New York, NY: Cambridge University Press, 1991.

LaVenia, Mark, Lora Cohen-Vogel, and Laura Lang. "The Common Core State Standards Initiative." *American Journal of Education* 121 (2015): 145–182.

Loertscher, David V., Koechlin, Carol, and Saudi Zwaan. *Ban those Bird Units: 15 Models for Teaching and Learning in Information-rich and Technology-rich Environments*. Salt Lake City, UT: Hi Willow Research and Publishing, 2005.

Loertscher, David V., and Laura H. Wimberley. *Collection Development Using the Collection Mapping Technique: A Guide for Librarians*. Salt Lake City, UT: High Willow Research and Publishing, 2009.

Longstreet, Wilma S., and Harold G. Shane. *Curriculum for the New Millennium*. Boston, MA: Allyn and Bacon, 1993.

Lunenburg, Fred C. "Theorizing about Curriculum: Conceptions and Definitions." *International Journal of Scholarly Academic Intellectual Diversity* 13 (2011): 1–6.

Maehr, Martin L., and Carol Midgley. *Transforming School Cultures*. Boulder, CO: Westview Press, 1996.

Mardis, Marsha A. "Collect or Curate?: Open Education Resources and the Future of the School Library Catalog." *School Library Monthly* 31 (2015): 29–31.

Marzano, Robert J., Timothy Waters, and Brian A. McNulty. *School Leadership that Works: From Research to Results*. Alexandria, VA: Association for Supervision and Curriculum Development (ASCD), 2005.

Matise, Miles. "The Enneagram: An Innovative Approach." *Journal of Professional Counseling Practice, Theory and Research* 35 (2007): 38–58.

MBTI website: https://www.cpp.com/products/mbti/index.aspx, 2016.

McGregor, Douglas. *The Human Side of Enterprise* (25th anniversary printing). New York, NY: McGraw-Hill, 1985.

McTighe, Jay, and Grant Wiggins. *Essential Questions: Opening Doors to Student Understanding*. Alexandria, VA: Association for Supervision and Curriculum Development, 2013.

Montiel-Overall Patricia. "Toward a Theory of Collaboration for Teachers and Librarians." *School Library Media Research* 8 (2005): n.p.

Morgan, Garth. *Images of Organization*. Thousand Oaks. CA: SAGE Publications, 1997.

Morris, Betty J. *Administering the School Library Media Center*. 5th ed. Denver, CO: Libraries Unlimited, 2010.

Myers, Isabel B. *Introduction to Type: A Guide to Understanding Your Results on the Myers-Briggs Type Indicator*. 6th ed. Gainesville, FL: Center for Applications of Psychological Type, 1998.

Myers, Isabel B. *Gifts Differing*. Palo Alto, CA: Consulting Psychologists Press, Inc., 1980.

Myers, Isabel B., and Paul Z. Myers. *Gifts Differing: Understanding Personality Type*. Mountain View, CA: Davies–Black Publishing, 1995.

Myers & Briggs Foundation. MBTI Basics. 2016. Retrieved from http://www.myers briggs.org/my-mbti-personality-type/mbti-basics/.

Nagowah, Leckraj, and Mauritius Soulakshmee Nagowah. "A Reflection on the Dominant Learning Theories: Behaviorism, Cognitivism and Constructivism." *The International Journal of Learning* 16 (2009): 279–285.

National School Reform Faculty (NSRF). Self-Guided Tour to NSRF Critical Friends Group. 2014. Retrieved from http://nsrf.iuserveit.org/sites/all/themes/NSRFtheme/assets/pdfs/Self-Guided%20Tour%201.0.pdf.

Oliva, Peter F. *Developing the Curriculum*. 7th ed. Boston, MA: Pearson, 2009.

Orlich, Donald C. "Educational Standards—Caveat Emptor." *Kappa Delta Pi Record* (2011): 52–57.

P21 Partnership for 21st Century Learning. n.d. Retrieved from http://www.p21.org/our-work/p21-framework.

Peters, Tom J., and Robert H. Waterman. *In Search of Excellence: Lessons from America's Best-run Companies*. New York, NY: HarpersCollins, 2004.

Peterson, Kent D., and Terrence E. Deal. "How Leaders Influence the Culture of Schools." *Educational Leadership* (1998): 28–30.

Purkey, Stewart C., and Marshall S. Smith. "Too Soon to Cheer? Synthesis of Research on Effective Schools." *Educational Leadership* (1982): 64–69.

Rifkin, Glenn. "Warren, G. Bennis, Scholar on Leadership, Dies 89." *New York Times,* B8. August 2014.

Riso Don R., and Russ Hudson. *Discovering Your Personality Type*. New York, NY: Houghton Mifflin Co., 2003.

Rogers, Everett M. *Diffusion of Innovations*. 5th ed. New York, NY: Free Press, 2003.

Roscello, Fran. "Standards our Earliest History: President's Column." *Knowledge Quest* 32 (2004): 6–8.

Schein, Edgar H. *Organizational Culture and Leadership*. 4th ed. San Francisco, CA: Jossey-Bass, Publishers, 2010.

Schein, Edgar H. *Organizational Culture and Leadership*. 2nd ed. San Francisco, CA: Jossey-Bass, Publishers, 1992.

Schreiber, Becky, and John Shannon. "Developing Leaders for the 21st Century." In *Leadership in the Library and Information Science Professions: Theory and Practice,* edited by Mark Winston, 35–60. New York, NY: Hawthorn Press, 2001.

Schreiber, Becky, and John Shannon. *Enneagram Workbook: Leading from any Position*. Corrales, NM: Schreiber Shannon Associates, 1998.

Schrio, Michael S. *Curriculum Theory: Conflicting Vision and Enduring Concerns.* Los Angeles, CA: Sage Publications, 2008.

Senge, Peter. *The Fifth Discipline: The Art and Practice of the Learning Organization.* New York: Doubleday Currency, 1990.

Shakespeare, William. *Romeo and Juliet.* New York, NY: Signet Classics, 1964.

Sheldon, Brooke E. *Leaders in Libraries: Styles and Strategies for Success.* Chicago, IL: American Library Association, 1991.

Shepard, Lorrie, Jane Hannaway, and Eva Baker. Eds. *Standards, Assessments, and Accountability: Education Policy White Paper.* Washington, D.C.: National Academy of Education, 2009.

Smirich, Linda. "Concepts of Culture and Organizational Analysis." *Administrative Science Quarterly* 28 (1983): 229–258.

Stripling, Barbara K. "Inquiry-based Learning." In *Curriculum Connections through the Library*, edited by Barbara K. Stripling and Sandra Hughes-Hassell, 3–39. Westport, CT: Libraries Unlimited, 2003.

Stripling, Barbara K., and Judy Pitts. *Brainstorms and Blueprints: Teaching Library Research as a Thinking Process.* Englewood, CO: Libraries Unlimited, 1988.

Stolp, Stephen. *Leadership for School Culture* (ERIC Digest 19). Eugene OR: University of Oregon/ERIC. (ERIC contract number ED-99-CO-0011), 1994.

Taba, Hilda. *Curriculum Development: Theory and Practice.* New York, NY: Harcourt, Brace & World, 1962.

Tallman, Joyce I., and Marilyn Z. Joyce. *Making the Writing and Research Connection with the I-Search Process.* New York, NY: Neal-Schuman Publishers, 2006.

Tanner, Daniel, and Laurel Tanner. *Curriculum Development: Theory into Practice.* 4th ed. Columbus OH: Pearson, Merrill Prentice Hall, 2007.

Traska, Maria R. District. "Library Supervisors under Duress: The Lilead Project Survey Results." 2014. Retrieved from: *americanlibrarymagazine.org.*

Udelhofen, Susan. *Keys to Curriculum Mapping: Strategies and Tools to Make It Work.* Thousand Oaks, CA: Corwin Press, 2005.

U.S. Department of Education. Every Student Succeeds Act (ESSA). 2015. Retrieved from www.ed.gov/essa?src=rn.

Wenger, Etienne. *Communities of Practice: Learning, Meaning and Identity.* Cambridge, NY: Cambridge University Press, 1998.

Wenger, Etienne, Richard McDermott, and William Snyder. *Cultivating Communities of Practice: A Guide to Managing Knowledge.* Boston, MA: Harvard Business School Press, 2002.

Wiggins, Grant, and Jay McTighe. *Understanding by Design.* Upper Saddle River, NJ: Merrill, Prentice Hall, 1998.

Wiggins, Grant, and Jay McTighe. *Understanding by Design.* 2nd ed. Upper Saddle River, NJ: Merrill, Prentice Hall, 2005.

Wiles, John, and Joseph C. Bondi. *Curriculum Development: A Guide to Practice.* 8th ed. New York, NY: Pearson, 2010.

Wilson, Leslie O. The Second Principle: The Work of Leslie Owen Wilson, Ed.D. 2016. Retrieved from: http://thesecondprinciple.com/instructional-design/types-of-curriculum/.

Woolls, Blanche. "When Leadership Is Followership: Comparing Practice and Theory in Library Education for Children's and School Librarians." In *Library Education and Leadership: Essays in Honor of Jane Anne Hannigan*, edited by Sheila S. Inter and Kay E. Vandergrift, 195–207. Metuchen, NJ: The Scarecrow Press, 1990.

Woolls, Blanche, Ann Weeks, and Sharon Coatney. *The School Library Manager.* 5th ed. Denver, CO: Libraries Unlimited, 2014.

Zmuda, Allison, Robert Kuklis, and Everett Kline. *Transforming Schools: Creating a Culture of Continuous Improvement.* Alexandria, VA: Association of Supervision and Curriculum Development (ASCD), 2004.

Zweizig, Douglas L., and Dianne McAfee Hopkins. *Lessons from Library Power: Enriching Teaching and Learning.* Englewood, CO: Libraries Unlimited, Inc., 1999.

Index

113

About the Author

JODY K. HOWARD, PhD, has educated school librarians and other library professionals at Palmer School of Library and Information Science, Old Dominion University, and Emporia State University. Her published works include numerous articles in the school library area, including "The Relationship between School Culture and the School Library Program: Four Case Studies." This article appeared in *School Library Research* and was selected as a top-twenty library instruction article of 2010 by the Library Instruction Round Table (LIRT). Howard received her doctorate in library and information management from Emporia State University.